GOING

Going On God's Way

ARTHUR WALLIS

KINGSWAY PUBLICATIONS
EASTBOURNE

Unless otherwise indicated, biblical quotations are from
the Holy Bible: New International Version, copyright ©
International Bible Society 1973, 1978, 1984.

RSV = Revised Standard Version
copyrighted 1946, 1952, © 1971, 1973 by the
Division of Christian Education of the National
Council of the Churches of Christ in the USA.

Front cover photo: Tony Stone Photolibrary—London

ISBN 0 85476 346 5

Printed in Great Britain for
KINGSWAY PUBLICATIONS LTD
Lottbridge Drove, Eastbourne, E. Sussex BN23 6NT by
BPCC Hazells Ltd
Member of BPCC Ltd

Contents

SECTION 3—LIVING IN THE WORLD

A Word about the Course

As a sequel to *Living God's Way*, the study course for new Christians, *Going on God's Way*, is to take the believer into the next stage of spiritual development. You will need a New International Version edition of the Bible, a notebook and a pencil.

The ground covered here is not so broad as in the earlier course. The emphasis is on personal growth and living for Christ in an alien society.

Living God's Way was designed for use in a local church setting where the new Christian is being personally discipled. This is not so important with *Going on God's Way*, and although it would be ideal to have someone older in the faith to take you through, you will gain much through working on your own. But do seek the help of a leader or older Christian if you are stuck with a problem.

With each study there is a memory verse. May I encourage you to embrace this self-discipline. If your memory is poor, this exercise will work wonders. And developing the habit of memorizing key scriptures will prove over the years to be a great blessing in your life. The best method is to write the memory verse (including the scripture reference) on a small card that you can slip in your pocket. If there is another version of the Bible that you are more familiar with than the NIV, memorize from that. And keep refreshing your memory on the verses you have learned. Constant rehearsing is the secret of memorizing.

The 'Home Task' tends to be practical rather than theoretical. Often it will demand more than simply finding answers to questions, and so acquiring head knowledge. You will need to seek God over the issues that are presented.

At the end of each study is an item called 'For Further Study'. This is to meet the insatiable appetite of those Oliver Twist students who always 'come back for more'. It's an optional extra, which is a little more demanding than the 'Home Task', with fewer references to guide your thinking.

May God bless you as you go through this course, bringing you into that spiritual maturity that has always been God's purpose for you since you came to Christ.

Introducing the Theme

'Fred, put your toys away and get ready for supper.'

No reply. A little more loudly, 'Did you hear what I said, Fred?'

'Don't want any supper,' mumbled Fred, continuing to play with his Lego.

'Whether you want it or not,' replied mother, 'put your toys away.'

You may think this is a typical exchange between mother and child until you learn that Fred is not an eight-year-old, but a young man of twenty-five, who is only eight years old mentally.

Alan was above average intelligence and keen to go to university. But you would never think that he had seen eighteen summers. He was less than five feet tall, with a round boyish face that had never felt the touch of a razor. His parents told me how concerned they were to find the treatment that would enable their boy to develop physically. What a heartache it is to the parents when the growth of their child is arrested mentally or physically.

Susan was strong-willed and stubborn. Her school-friends found it hard to cope with her tantrums and her self-centredness. Three years ago she was converted to Christ. Now she goes to meetings instead of discos, but in lots of ways she's the same old Sue. She's had plenty of teaching, but is still an up-and-down type of Christian. Her friends still find her self-willed and lapsing into moodiness if she doesn't have her way. She's picked up the spiritual jargon very well, can pray quite nicely and talk about spiritual things, but her behaviour is not all that different from her unbelieving friends. If she is born into God's family she is certainly not growing up.

There are many children of God like this who are a heartache to their heavenly Father.

Often there is nothing that medical science can do for the mentally and physically retarded. But what about those who are spiritually backward? Is this like a club foot—something that you're born with and have to live with? No, that is not what the Bible teaches. God is not a tyrant. He doesn't set us a standard that we cannot keep, or give us commands that we cannot obey. He gives us grace to grow, and expects us to do so. Whatever our background, upbringing or temperament, he holds us responsible for our immaturity.

If we are stunted believers we will lose out both in time and in eternity. We will deprive the church and the world of the blessing that we would have been, had we matured. But more importantly, we shall thwart God's purpose in saving us, and rob him of his portion in our lives.

In our opening study we shall take a close look at the symptoms of spiritual immaturity. That should help us to discover where we are. Then in Section 1 we will consider what the Christian is as *The New Person in Christ*, and how we may develop in every area of our renewed being. Section 2, *Growing Strong in God*, will touch a number of very practical areas that vitally affect our spiritual growth. Finally, in Section 3 *Living in the World*, we face the fact that the environment in which we are called to live for God is not 'home' to us. In fact it is antagonistic to the claims of Christ. But God has designed that this is the setting in which we are to fulfil our calling. Amazingly, he uses it to hone us, shape us and mature us for our heavenly destiny.

Facing our Immaturity

Read
Hebrews 5:11—6:3.

Signs of immaturity

God's simple plan for his children is that the crisis of *new birth* is followed by the process of *spiritual growth*, leading to a state of *spiritual maturity*. But it is possible for the process to be arrested. The Christians addressed in our reading, although truly born into God's family, had not grown up spiritually or become mature. They were behaving like spiritual babies. No one minds if a twelve-month-old toddler is constantly falling over, dribbling, spitting out his food, or bursting into tears. But what if a teenager behaved like this? The writer of the Hebrews epistle knew that these believers were not growing up in their spiritual understanding because he was finding it hard to teach them anything more than their spiritual ABC, which he calls 'elementary truths' (5:12). No wonder he was urging them: 'Go on to maturity' (6:1).

It is serious enough not to be growing, but even more serious when we do not recognize that this is so. It is possible to be gaining knowledge about the Bible, talking or even praying in spiritual language, and yet not be really growing. This passage gives us five marks of spiritual immaturity.

1. Having to lay again the foundation of repentance

The writer tells these Christians that not only are they not yet ready for more advanced teaching, but that they need to learn their ABC all over again (5:12).

A few verses later (6:1) he tells them that he wants them to be able to leave their ABC 'and go on to maturity, *not laying again the foundation of repentance*' (my italics). He was likening their Christian lives to a building under construction, with repentance as part of the foundation. It seems that they were constantly having to dig up the foundation and lay it again, so that after all this time the building had made little progress.

Let's take repentance. Do you find that the same old temptations are flooring you? That you are having to repent over and over again for the same sins? This could mean that your foundation of repentance has not been laid thoroughly; you may be using the right words as you confess your sins to God, but are you repenting from the heart and really turning away from that sin? This is a common mark of immaturity.

2. Unable to share the truth with others

'By this time you ought to be teachers' (5:12) says the writer. Was he being a bit tough on these Christians? No, he is not saying that they should all be able to teach a congregation. He is saying that part of growing up spiritually is that we become confident about what we have learned, and *able to share it* personally with others.

It is not just teachers, preachers or leaders who are called to share in this sense. It is something God wants all his children to be able to do. (See Hebrews 3:13 and 10:25.) The word 'encourage' in these scriptures may also mean 'exhort'. 1 Thessalonians 5:11 says the same thing, and teaches us that our sharing in this way will 'build each other up'.

Let's look at an example. Meeting a fellow Christian in the street who I know is going through a tough patch, I share with him the thought that God doesn't always or immediately change our circumstances, but he says, 'My grace is sufficient for you' (2 Cor 12:9). In other words, God's resources are available to give him victory in the situation. A very simple thought, but God speaks through it, and the Christian goes on his way strengthened and encouraged.

3. *Unable to take solids*

'You need milk, not solid food' (v.12) says the writer. He felt that these Christians had known the Lord long enough to be able to understand the more advanced teaching he was bringing them, but they were saying, 'It's too deep. We can't understand it. Please just give us the simple truths of the gospel.'

Here then is another test of whether you are growing spiritually. Do you only have an appetite for the simple truths that you learned when you first came to Christ— that Jesus died for your sins, that you have eternal life, that he has gone to prepare a home for you in heaven, etc.? Or do you find that you are able to manage a much more solid diet without suffering spiritual indigestion? If not, do believe that as you go through these studies, God will enable you to digest the solid food that it will contain.

4. *Unable to use the word of righteousness*

'Not acquainted with the teaching about righteousness' (v.13) is better rendered, 'Unskilled in the word of righteousness' (RSV). This has the thought of Scripture being a tool or a weapon that these believers should have

15

been trained to handle. The fact that this was not so was another mark of their immaturity.

They did not know how to use the word in meditation, and so feed themselves spiritually. They did not know how to use it to instruct and help others with their problems. They did not know how to use it to bring comfort to those who were sad, or counsel to those who were perplexed. They did not know how to use it in intercession, by pleading its promises with God. They did not know how to wield it as 'the sword of the Spirit' (Eph 6:17) to drive back the attacks of Satan.

Ability to handle the word of God practically is an important part of becoming mature. Pray that as you go through this course, God will make you skilful in using the word of righteousness.

5. *Unable to distinguish good from evil*

The Hebrew passage tells us that the mature 'by constant use have trained themselves to distinguish good from evil' (v.14). The one who is immature is not able to do this, and so may easily be influenced and led astray.

A business friend persuades a young Christian to join him in a business venture which looks very attractive, but is not fully honest. He falls for this temptation because he is not able to discern wrong. Someone comes to a believer's front door with what seems to be sound Bible teaching, and leaves him literature. It all seems right and reasonable, but he fails to detect the falsehood. Scripture warns us not to be led astray by 'false teachers' who will bring in 'destructive heresies' (2 Pet 2:1).

Paul teaches something very similar when he speaks of us all becoming mature: 'Then we will no longer be infants, tossed back and forth by the waves, and blown here and there by every wind of teaching and by the cunning and craftiness of men in their deceitful scheming' (Eph 4:14). When a young Christian is 'tossed back and forth' by various teachings he becomes unstable and insecure. In the early years of our Christian life, older Christians will be able to protect us and guide us in these areas, but we must not be satisfied to remain spiritual toddlers who need to be watched at every turn. We must grow up.

How you hear is the key

We have looked at the marks which showed that these Christians were not growing up, but what was the reason? The answer is found in the opening verse of our reading. It says that they were 'slow to learn'. Older versions translate this more literally as, 'dull of hearing'. That did not mean *that they needed a hearing aid!* It has to do with the spiritual ear which enables the heart (rather than the head) to hear and understand. Jesus often spoke of this kind of hearing (Mt 13:9; Rev 2:7). It did not mean *that they had not had the right teaching*. They had in fact been well taught the ABC of the Christian life, but had not properly taken it in. It did not mean *that they were lacking in human intelligence*. Natural wisdom is not the key to spiritual understanding. See what Jesus had to say about this (Mt 11:25–26).

Is your hearing of God's word sharp or dull? This decides whether or not you are really growing up. Let us look at the parable of the sower (Lk 8:5–15). Some of his seed fell along the path, some on rocky ground, some among thorns and some on good soil, all with differing results. This parable is not to teach us how to scatter the seed, but how to receive the seed, that is, *how to hear* the word of God. Jesus explained (vv.11–15) that the four different soils that received the seed picture how different people *hear* the word (vv.18–23).

The well-trodden path pictures the *hard heart* that doesn't respond to God's word. The rocky ground speaks of the *unbelieving heart*. The ground is so full of the rocks of unbelief that there is little room for the soil of faith. The thorny patch speaks of the *divided heart*, which is affected by life's worries, riches and pleasures. These smother or suffocate the good seed that tries to grow up. Of these, Jesus says, 'They do not mature' (v.14). Finally, the good soil speaks of the *noble and good heart* that produces a crop.

What we learn from this parable is that it is the state of our hearts that determines how we hear. If you have been listening to God's word but not growing, then it has something to do with your spiritual hearing. No wonder Jesus concluded the parable with these important words, 'Take heed then *how you hear*' (v.18 RSV). This is what we shall do in the second part of our home task.

Memorize

Therefore let us leave the elementary teachings about Christ and go on to maturity (Heb 6:1).

Home task

1. Look first at those five marks of immaturity. Write down in your notebook which of them you feel are true of you. If you believe God is going to use this course to help you to grow up, then confess that to him now. It is always important to confess what we believe. Now take these marks of immaturity to God one by one, asking him that before you have completed this course you will begin to change in each of these areas.

18

2. Turn again to the parable of the sower in Luke 8:5–15. Write down in your notebook what Jesus said about each kind of soil. It will not be so easy to recognize which soil (or soils) is a picture of your heart. The reason for this is given in Jeremiah 17:9. The heart is so deceitful it can even deceive its owner. But the way through is given in verse 10. Instead of trying to search your own heart, let God do it for you. Pray the prayer of David in Psalm 139:23–24, and believe for change.

For further study

'Unable to use the word of righteousness' was one sign of immaturity we noted in these Hebrew Christians. We saw that God's word was like a tool or weapon that could be used in several ways. Make a note of these. It is a good idea to have a notebook handy when you read the Bible, and to write out in full the scriptures you come across under headings like these. In this way you can build up a compendium of useful scriptures that will help you to be skilled, and not 'unskilled in the word of righteousness'. Let's make a start.

We can make valuable use of 'the word of righteousness' by pleading the prayer promises in our intercession. Read John 14—16 and then:

1. Note down all the asking promises Jesus gave.

2. Note how many times he said that we must ask 'in his name'.

3. What do you think this means? Give practical examples.

SECTION 1

The New Person

A Man in Christ

Read
John 14:15–21 and 15:1–10.

Introduction

'In Christ' was a favourite expression of Paul the apostle, and he was the only New Testament writer to use the expression 'Christ in you'. But what do these phrases really mean? 'In Christ' is another way of describing a Christian. Paul describes himself as 'a man in Christ' (2 Cor 12:2). Earlier in that same letter he had said, 'If anyone is in Christ, he is a new creation; the old has gone, the new has come' (2 Cor 5:17). But we will discover that these expressions tell us much more—something of what it really means to be a Christian.

Jesus said it first

It was not Paul, but Christ, who first spoke in this way, saying to his disciples, 'You are in me, and I am in you.' It was on that last night before he went to the cross. He was preparing his disciples for that moment when he would be forcibly taken from them. He promised that the Holy Spirit would come to them (Jn 14:16) and that

23

he would more than fill the enormous gap left by his departure. He wanted them to know that the sacred relationship he now had with them was not about to end, but would shortly enter an even more wonderful phase.

It was at this point that Jesus made three mysterious statements that the disciples would have found difficult to understand. In the first he said, 'Before long, the world will not see me any more, but you will see me' (v.19). He was promising them *spiritual sight*. Then he said, 'Because I live, you also will live.' That meant a supply of *spiritual life*. And finally he said, 'On that day you will realise that I am in my Father, and you are in me, and I am in you.' That pointed to a *spiritual union*.

Before we look at these three statements of Jesus, did you notice how the last one commenced? 'On that day...'. What day was he referring to? Look back to verses 16–17, and you will see that he had been telling them about the coming of the Holy Spirit. So 'On that day' was the day of Pentecost, when the Holy Spirit would come on these disciples. Pentecost is not only a past event, but a present experience. Have you had that experience? Has the Holy Spirit come on you? If not, ask the friend who is taking you through this course, or someone else that you know, to help you and pray with you for this. Promises like Luke 11:13, John 7:37–39 and Acts 1:8 are there for you to claim. You cannot experience the full reality of what Jesus is saying here without that experience.

Spiritual sight

What Jesus was saying was that when he had gone they would still see him—with the eye of faith. This is one of the wonderful characteristics of our relationship with Christ. Though we do not see him physically, he is as real to us as if we did. It is by faith that we have this spiritual sight. Said Peter, 'Even though you do not see him now [physically], you *believe* in him and are filled with an inexpressible and glorious joy' (1 Pet 1:8). The world may say, 'Seeing is believing,' but the Christian declares, 'Believing is seeing.' If you lose sight of Jesus, or if your vision of him becomes dim, you are certainly suffering from defective faith, and you will need to enquire what the reason is. With renewed faith comes renewed vision. It's vision that makes Jesus real.

Spiritual life

'Because I live, you also will live.' How often he had warned these disciples of his coming death, and promised that he would rise again. But they had been too scared to take it in. Now he was telling them that this resurrection life would not be for him alone, but for them too. How important it was for them to know that fact when witnessing to a hostile world. It is equally important for us. Notice how Paul prayed for the believers of his day:

> That the eyes of your heart may be enlightened [that's spiritual sight] in order that you may know...his incomparably great power *for us who believe*. That power is like the working of his mighty strength, which he exerted in Christ when he raised him from the dead' (Eph 1:18–20, italics mine).

Notice that this power is 'for us who believe'. 'God... made us alive with Christ' by the same resurrection power (Eph 2:1–5). That was when we were born again.

Perhaps you say, 'Yes, I've had that experience, but it's keeping it up that bothers me.' It's here that the words of Jesus are so reassuring. He is telling them that they would continue to enjoy the flow of his resurrection life. In effect he is saying, 'Because I go on living, you will go on living too, by my resurrection life.' Perhaps the disciples were thinking to themselves, 'It sounds wonderful, but how will it work?' Jesus went on to explain.

Spiritual union

'On that day you will realise that I am in my Father, and you are in me, and I am in you.' On that day, when the Holy Spirit came to teach them, they would fully understand. One thing was clear; he was telling them, 'You will have the same relationship with me as I have had with my Father. Just as I have been in my Father, so you will be in me.' Wow! That relationship he enjoyed with his Father was something they had watched with envy all the time they had been with him. God seemed so close, so real to him. Just to think that they could now have that kind of relationship with him!

Jesus then, as he so often did, went on to make use of picture language. He used the wonderful parable of the vine and the branches (chapter 15) to explain this new relationship. It illustrates perfectly our union with Christ.

A vine-branch relationship

He had said, 'Because I live, you also will live.' Now he says, 'I am the vine; you are the branches' (v.5). Do the branches have any expectation of life apart from the vine? Could they continue to live if the vine died? Now we begin to see the truth that we share in Christ's resurrection (Col 3:1). No problem here of keeping it up. In the words of an old hymn:

> Moment by moment I'm kept in his love,
> Moment by moment I've life from above.

Notice that Jesus didn't say, 'I am the trunk,' but, 'I am the vine.' In fact a vine has very little trunk, it's nearly all branches. Jesus is the whole vine, and when we are born again we are united with him and become part of him. Is it not true that the branches are in the vine and that the vine is in the branches? It is equally true that we are in Christ and that he is in us.

Since we are part of Christ, 'we have come to share in Christ' (Heb 3:14). Just as all that there is in the vine is for the branches, so all that there is in Jesus is for us. Scripture says that all the fullness of God dwells in him (Col 1:19), and that that fullness is available to us (Col 2:9–10)—all that we shall ever need to live the Christian life. John the apostle spoke about it when he said, 'From the fullness of his grace we have all received one blessing after another' (Jn 1:16).

The one purpose

This wonderful relationship between vine and branch is not to make the branches feel good or get them 'all blessed up'. Jesus said that his Father was the gardener (v.1). Why does a gardener take so much trouble to cultivate his vine? He wants grapes. Count how many times 'fruit' occurs in verse 1–16. But what is fruit? All fruit is the product of life, and the fruit that God wants can only come from the life of Jesus flowing through us. God is looking for *the fruit of Christian character* (Gal 5:22–23)—what we *are* in Christ. He is also looking for *the fruit of Christian service* (Col 1:6, 10)—what we *do* for Christ.

Maintain the union

According to Jesus the one who *remains* in him bears fruit (v.4). That word remain (or abide) occurs again and again in the parable. It is the key to our part in the fruit-bearing process. If you as a Christian are not bearing fruit, what, according to this verse, are you failing to do?

To the command, 'Remain in me,' Jesus adds by way of explanation, 'No branch can bear fruit by itself.' For the first years of my Christian life I tried hard to prove that Jesus was mistaken. As a Christian surely I could now bear fruit. I must pray a little more, read the Bible more often, try a little harder. God had to use the discipline of failure to bring me to that cry of desperation, 'Oh, God, I can't.' Only then could I see that nothing but his life flowing through me, as the sap flows out to the branches, could produce fruit.

I began to understand what union with Christ really meant—a life of dependence on him for everything. 'Remain in me' could only mean maintain this living union by an attitude of trust. I saw how often an attitude of 'we've got what it takes', had replaced a childlike trust. I could see it was faith that released the 'life sap', and unbelief that cut it off. See how even Paul had to learn this lesson of his own weakness and of God's wonderful sufficiency (2 Cor 12:9).

Memorize

Remain in me, and I will remain in you. No branch can bear fruit by itself; it must remain in the vine. Neither can you bear fruit unless you remain in me (Jn 15:4).

Home task

1. John 15:2 speaks of God as the Gardener pruning fruitful branches. In what ways does he do this (Jn 15:3;

Eph 5:25–26; Heb 12:9–11)? Note down any experiences you have had of this pruning operation—and what you believe it has accomplished. Follow the psalmist and acknowledge God's goodness in this (Ps 119:66–68).

2. Read about two disciples of Christ in Luke 10: 38–42. Compare them with the two kinds of believer Jesus talked about in John 15: the one that remains in Christ and produces fruit, and the one who does not. Write down in your notebook the reasons why you think Jesus commended Mary, rather than Martha. Would you qualify for Mary's commendation?

3. We saw that the greatest hindrance to maintaining our union with Christ is an attitude of independence and self-sufficiency, and that God uses the discipline of failure to make us realize it. Write down what you think is the cause of this attitude in us, and how we should deal with it. (If, after a good think, you are without ideas, see if you find Proverbs 16:18 and 1 Peter 5:6 helpful.)

For further study

We saw that even Paul had to come to a place where he acknowledged his weakness and dependence on God. Turn to Romans 7:14–25 where he describes his struggle with indwelling sin. Note the verses in which he speaks of his perplexity as to why he behaved the way he did.

1. Write out the verse in which he acknowledges his total inability to live a life that pleases God. Compare this with two statements Jesus made in John 15:4–5.

2. Write out the verse that records his desperate cry for deliverance.

3. Turn on to chapter 8 verses 1–4 and describe in your own words the great deliverance he discovered.

The Mind Renewed

Read
Romans 12:1–3.

That think tank

There's a little verse that says of man, 'For as he thinks within himself, so he is' (Prov 23:7, New American Standard Bible).

Someone has put it this way:

> You are not what you think you are,
> But what you think—you are!

In other words, if we had some electrical device that could throw our thought lives on to a screen for all to see, everyone would know what kind of people we are. Ouch!

Our minds are the seedplot of our lives. 'Sow a thought, reap an act. Sow an act, reap a habit. Sow a habit, reap a character. Sow a character, reap a destiny.' No wonder that when Satan attacked Adam and Eve in the Garden of Eden, he aimed first at their minds, sowing distrust in their thinking about God (Gen 3:4–5). And he is still at the same game.

The mind needs converting

Since our minds, as well as every other part of us, were marred by sin, it is not surprising that salvation involves a complete turn about in our thinking. Scripture tells us that the mind of the unbeliever is:

(a) Defiled and corrupted (Tit 1:15).

(b) Blinded by Satan (2 Cor 4:4).

(c) Hostile towards God (Col 1:21).

Despite all this, through the gospel God appeals to men's intellect. He says, 'Come now, let us reason together' (Is 1:18). He wants men to know that 'the good news' is neither unreasonable nor illogical. Sometimes the seed falls on hard ground and the devil snatches it away. That's when men hear, but don't understand (Mt 13:19). Salvation doesn't call for blind faith, but reasoned faith.

In the change of mind that takes place at conversion man has his part to play and God has his. Man is required to *repent*, which means to rethink. It's more than saying 'sorry'. It's a change of mind leading to a change of course. He obeys the call, 'Let the wicked forsake his way and the evil man his thoughts (Is 55:7). God, for his part, promises, 'I will put my law in their minds and write it on their hearts' (Jer 31:33). So before we start living God's way we have to start thinking God's way.

This is the beginning of what the Bible calls 'the renewing of your mind' (Rom 12:2). New birth has to be followed by spiritual growth, and that includes our renewed minds. Paul tells us, 'Stop thinking like children...but in your thinking be adults' (1 Cor 14:20). Think of your mind as a garden. Remember how neglected and out of hand it was when the Lord Jesus took possession of this property he had purchased. Things have changed, haven't they? But, I'm sure you will agree, there's still a lot more renewing needed. Both clearing and planting are called for.

Clear the ground

We are told to gird up our minds (1 Pet 1:13, RSV). In Bible lands the loose flowing robes of the Oriental had to be gathered at the waist with a girdle before he could walk, work or fight, otherwise he would trip. This was 'girding up the loins'. It means dealing with what hinders or impedes us. So the NIV rightly translates Peter's phrase, 'Prepare your minds for action.' Deal with the negative things that hinder right thinking. In gardening terms, we mean clear the ground for planting. Let's look at three poisonous weeds we need to tackle.

1. Impure thoughts

Do they matter? Yes, because thoughts produce actions, habits and character, as we have said. Jesus said, 'Anyone who looks at a woman lustfully has already committed adultery with her in his heart' (Mt 5:28). He wasn't implying that the thought is as bad as the act, but that the thought is where sin begins, so it must be nipped in the bud. This word of Jesus reminds us that Satan often uses our eyes to attack us with unclean thoughts. See how he did this with Potiphar's wife (Gen 39:7) and later with King David (2 Sam 11:2–4). Peter speaks of those who have 'eyes full of adultery' (2 Pet 2:14).

There is, of course, always forgiveness and cleansing when we confess impure thoughts, but prevention is better than cure. Job solved this problem by setting a guard on his eyes (Job 31:1). For us that would mean saying 'no' to certain paperbacks, glossy magazines and late-night movies—things that we know are calculated to stir up sexual desire.

Even when we avoid these, unclean thoughts may spring up unbidden in our minds. They are not sin if we reject them at once. Someone has said. 'You can't stop a bird alighting on your head, but you can stop it making a nest in your hair!'

2. Anxious thoughts

Worry is a form of fear, and Jesus dealt with fear on the cross, when he dealt with all our sins (Heb 2:14). So there is full deliverance from this destructive weed. We are not to make excuses: 'I take after Mum, and she's the worrying sort!' As believers we are under command: 'Do not be anxious!' 'Not even over something very important?' 'Do not be anxious *about anything*, but in *everything*...present your requests to God. And the peace of God...will guard your hearts and your minds in Christ Jesus' (Phil 4:6–7, italics mine).

We could summarize the above statement by saying, 'Turn your anxieties into prayer until the peace of God takes over.' Indulging in worry is indulging in unbelief. Handing over the situation to God in prayer is acting in faith. In this way we cultivate a steadfast faith. We can tell God with confidence, 'You will keep in perfect peace him whose mind is steadfast, because he trusts in you' (Is 26:3).

3. Earthbound thoughts

God knows that we are human beings with physical bodies that have to be clothed, fed and housed. We are not to be careless or unconcerned about material things. But nor are we to behave like unbelievers, whose minds are dominated by earthly things. 'For the pagans,' Jesus reminded us, 'run after all these things.' Instead we, who have a different set of values, are to 'seek first his kingdom' (Mt 6:32–33). Paul even stated that one mark of certain men, who were 'enemies of the cross', was that 'their mind is on earthly things' (Phil 3:18–19).

The Bible never suggests that material things are sinful. It is just our attitude to them that may be sinful. We are not to feel guilty about that which 'God... richly provides... for our enjoyment' (1 Tim 6:17). But since the cross has freed us from being bound to material possessions, and given us a heavenly goal, God's word exhorts us, 'Set your minds on things above, not on earthly things' (Col 3:2).

If our minds are to be renewed we must not only 'clear the ground', but also:

Plant the garden

'Nature abhors a vaccum.' If you clear the weeds but fail to plant out the beds, the weeds will reappear and grow even more vigorously. We spoke of not letting impure thoughts roost in the belfry of our minds, but Paul goes even further. He says, 'Whatever is true, whatever is noble, whatever is right, whatever is pure, whatever is lovely... think about such things (Phil 4:8). This is how we plant out the garden. But where is this 'food for thought' to be found? Primarily in God's word.

'Let the word of Christ dwell in you richly as you teach and admonish one another' (Col 3:16). So reading and meditating on the Bible is the way to fill your mind with 'God thoughts', and thus plant the garden.

Paul describes the minds of certain unbelievers that, 'their thinking became futile and their foolish hearts were darkened' (Rom 1:21). Futility and foolishness—that would have pretty well described the minds of all of us, till we were born again and made 'wise for salvation' (2 Tim 3:15). But that change from foolishness to wisdom when we received salvation is a process that goes on as we fill our minds with the truth.

This does not mean reading the Bible as if you were swotting for a Geography exam. It is not just filling your mind with biblical facts. Facts will teach you more *about* God, but that is not *knowing God*. How you plant the garden is vital. Letting the word dwell in you richly requires *faith*, that as you read, or listen to the word of God being read or explained, the Holy Spirit will give you that inner understanding that the Bible calls *revelation*. Do you remember that verse or truth that suddenly lit up for you? That was revelation. See how Paul prayed that the Ephesian Christians would have this (Eph 1:17–18). I pray for this continually, especially in connection with my Bible reading. You do the same, and the garden of your mind will surely be planted.

Memorize

> *Do not conform any longer to the pattern of this world, but be transformed by the renewing of your mind. Then you will be able to test and approve what God's will is—his good, pleasing and perfect will* (Rom 12:2).

Home task

1. Many Christians still have the mistaken notion that the thought life of the believer doesn't matter very much. Write down in your notebook the reasons why you think it is very important. Here are some more Scriptures that will help you to fill out your answer: Genesis 6:5; 1 Chronicles 28:9; Psalm 139:1–2; 1 Corinthians 13:11.

2. Let's have a ground-clearing exercise. We have only mentioned a few of the many poisonous weeds that

spring up in the garden of the mind. There may be others that you are conscious of. Pray David's prayer in Psalm 139:23–24. Ask God to show you all the weeds he sees. Confess them one by one, and be sure to receive by faith his promised forgiveness and cleansing (1 Jn 1:9). Then start the planting out. If it was proud thoughts you confessed, ask him to clothe you with the humility of Jesus. Make an entry in your notebook of these new plants. It will be useful to look over them later on and see how they have been growing.

For further study

1. 'You are not what you think you are.' What *do* you think of yourself? Consider two constrasting but accurate assessments Paul made of himself (2 Cor 11:5; 1 Tim 1:15) and his counsel to us (Rom 12:3).

2. Study the contrast between the spiritual mind and the unspiritual or fleshly mind (Rom 8:5–9; Col 2:18–19).

3. We are exhorted to have the attitude or mind-set of Christ (Phil 2:5–11). Consider what this attitude is, how you cultivate it and how it would affect your relationship with others (vv.2–4).

4. Loving God involves our minds as well as our hearts and our souls (Mt 22:37). What does that mean practically?

Controlled Emotions

Read
Isaiah 61:1–3.

Understanding emotions

An emotion is 'a mental feeling', so the theme is closely linked with our previous study. Note that:

1. God has emotions

Love is the very essence of his being (1 Jn 4:16), but he also hates (Prov 6:16). We read of God being joyful (Zeph 3:17), jealous (Ex 34:14) and angry (Deut 1:37). Since we are made in his image (Gen 1:27) it is not surprising that we are emotional creatures.

2. People vary emotionally

The measure in which we experience the same basic emotions, and the measure in which we express them vary greatly. This may be due to our sex (men being generally less emotional than women), nationality, culture and even experiences we have had in life.

3. The Christian life is emotional

Again, this varies with us all. From the time we first

experience conviction of sin, which pricks our consciences (Acts 26:14) and disturbs our peace, through the new birth experience where the love of God is poured into our hearts (Rom 5:5) to a 'believing' which Peter calls being 'filled with an inexpressible and glorious joy' (1 Pet 1:8)—all this could hardly be described as unemotional.

4. Our bodies are involved

In the first place emotional stress can bring on sickness or exhaustion. Doctors tell us that bitterness can bring on arthritis, tension can cause ulcers or back problems, and so on. But on the other side of the coin, mental and physical exhaustion can deeply affect our emotions. After his spectacular victory on Mount Carmel Elijah sank into deep depression, asking God to take away his life (1 Kings 19:4). This would not only have been due to a sense of failure (running for his life at the threat of Jezebel), but also to physical and mental exhaustion after the dramatic events recorded in the previous chapter (note verse 46). For emotional stability we should avoid over-taxing our bodies.

Emotions need to be released

God has not given us emotions to be repressed, but to be released. This is a real emotional need with many, especially in the West.

1. The example of Scripture

Orientals are much less inhibited. We even see this as we look at the believers in the New Testament. They were much freer than most of us in expressing their love for one another, their joys and their sorrows (Acts 20:36–38; 1 Thess 5:26). We see this in a character as manly and rugged as that of Paul (2 Cor 2:4; Phil 4:10).

2. Facing inhibitions

Emotions stifled or bottled up, especially in infancy or childhood, usually result in spritual inhibition. My wife used to be a bad sailor. Even before the boat left the quayside she would feel queasy. She was being prayed for by a friend who knew nothing of this. Suddenly she said, 'I see a little girl in a boat looking at the deep water. She is very afraid, but dare not tell anyone.' My wife did not know she had this repressed fear, and could not remember the incident, but from that moment she was released, and even a rough voyage was no problem. Natural emotions, such as sorrow at the loss of a loved one, need to find free expression. Tears help the healing process.

3. The Spirit-baptism factor

Most who have known the experience of the baptism in the Holy Spirit and the exercise of spiritual gifts testify to a real and valuable release in their emotional life. Some speak of being 'all screwed up inside' before they received the Holy Spirit. Others describe their receiving as 'falling in love with Jesus for the first time' (see Romans 5:5). This emotional factor that causes some to fear, or even reject this experience, is often the very thing they need.

Emotions must be controlled

If emotions are not to be repressed, as we have said, they are certainly to be controlled. God puts a high premium on this (Prov 16:32). It determines whether we are wise or foolish (Prov 29:11). Failure to control emotions could be more serious than repressing them.

1. The devil gets a foothold

If we give free rein to such emotions as temper, lust and jealousy, we may open the door to demonic activity in our lives. Paul warns us of this: 'In your anger do not sin. Do not let the sun go down while you are still angry.' In other words, bring it under control, and so, 'Do not give the devil a foothold' (Eph 4:26–27).

2. Some biblical examples

After David slew Goliath, the women, as they greeted the returning soldiers, praised David more than King Saul. Saul was angry and jealous (1 Sam 18:6–9). This opened the door yet further to demonic activity in his life and led to the first of many murderous attacks on David (vv.10–11).

Another case: Amnon, son of David, fell in love with Tamar, his half-sister. Lust took over, and he raped her. Immediatey love turned to hate—a characteristic mark of demonic activity (2 Sam 13:8–15). Later Amnon was murdered in revenge by Tamar's brother, Absalom.

These examples illustrate another kind of wisdom than that of the self-controlled man we noticed in Proverbs—a wisdom that is 'earthly, unspiritual, of the devil' (Jas 3:15).

Ruling our emotions

From a spiritual point of view emotions may be positive, negative or neutral. We need not concern ourselves here with the positive, such as love, joy and peace which are the fruit of the Spirit. Negative emotions, like the biblical examples we have just considered, are the reactions of our fallen nature, and must be handled very firmly. The neutral ones are human reactions, as with the sorrow of bereavement, the joy at some piece of good news, or depression through sickness or disappointment. Although these are not to be suppressed, they do need to be controlled.

1. Handling sinful emotions

In dealing with a whole range of behavioural patterns that belong to our old way of life, including emotions, Paul calls us to take radical action. He says, 'Get rid of all bitterness, rage and anger' (Eph 4:31). He says, 'Put to death, therefore, whatever belongs to your earthly nature: sexual immorality, impurity, lust' (Col 3:5). But how?

(a) Confess the source from which any ungodly emotion comes—that earthly sinful nature (see above).

(b) Renounce it before God. Do it audibly.

(c) Then, acknowledging that Jesus dealt with this at the cross, confess by faith that you have now 'crucified the sinful nature with its passions and desires' (Gal 5:24).

(d) Since the Holy Spirit as well as nature 'abhors a vacuum', seal the whole transaction by putting on by faith those spiritual emotions which are the opposite of those that you have just put off: 'Clothe yourselves with compassion, kindness, humility...' (Col 3:12).

2. Controlling natural emotions

Although it is healthy and good for these to have a normal outlet, they may easily take over and so become a spiritual hindrance. For example, to be downcast for a while through difficult circumstances is natural, but if we don't snap out of it the way David did (Ps 42:5), we may sink into deep depression and our testimony will be affected. A time of joy and exuberance of spirits must not go off into an emotional 'high' because this is almost always followed by an emotional 'low'. Nor must sorrow

43

be allowed to overwhelm us (2 Cor 2:7). This is where we are to stand out as different from the world. Our sorrow is hope-filled (1 Thess 4:13) while that of the world is death-filled (2 Cor 7:10). But if these are natural emotions that we are talking about, however will we manage to control them?

(a) We must recognize that we are no longer merely natural people but spiritual people (2 Cor 5:17) and have access to spiritual resources that natural people do not have.

(b) When we yield ourselves to God then our whole being, spirit, soul and body—and that must include our emotions—come under the rule of the Spirit. And 'the fruit of the Spirit is . . . self-control' (Gal 5:22–23).

(c) We must commit any uncontrolled emotion to God, and believe for the grace of the Holy Spirit to control it. If we cannot get through on this we may be in need of emotional healing. We will touch on this in our final section as we turn our eyes on—

Jesus—our pattern and our physician

The emotional life of Jesus provides us with:

1. Our perfect pattern

It was strong, rich and varied, but always under perfect control. Although it was predicted that he would be '*a man of sorrows*' (Is 53:3), we only read of two occasions where Jesus wept in public (Lk 19:41; Jn 11:35). However, it would seem that tears, even 'loud cries' characterized his private prayer life (Heb 5:7). But he never allowed his sorrows to bring heaviness to the company he was in. This must have been because of *the joy that always characterized him*, even when facing the cross (Heb 12:2). Paul spoke of being 'sorrowful, yet always rejoicing' (2 Cor 6:10), and Jesus demonstrated this perfectly. God had anointed him with 'the oil of joy' above his companions (Heb 1:9). When Jesus spoke to his disciples of his joy being in them, they knew he was promising them something very real and very wonderful (Jn 15:11).

Then there was *his amazing love and compassion*, not only for his own (Jn 13:1), but also for his enemies (see Lk 23:34). Compassion is that feeling of pity and deep sympathy towards those in need. Often we read of him being moved with compassion as he looked at the crowds in their need or the sick in their distress (Mt 9:36, 20:34). But note *the striking absence of negative emotions*. Though at times he displayed righteous anger at men's stubbornness, unbelief or hypocrisy, he never had an outburst of temper. He was without bitterness or jealousy, and he never gave way to self-pity, or discouragement, moodiness or irritability. The only fear he knew was the fear of the Lord. He has sent the Holy Spirit to make us like him.

2. *Our divine physician*

He did not come simply to leave us with an unattainable standard to follow, but also to touch us and make us whole, in our emotions as in everything else. He knows and understands our inner wounds and bruises, that 'crushed spirit' (Prov 17:22), or those feelings of inferiority or rejection. We may, indeed we *must*, open up these areas to him. Was he not sent to 'bind up the broken-hearted' (Is 61:1)? We may need the help of a mature Spirit-filled Christian here, but we must not settle for anything less than the wholeness Christ came to bring.

Memorize

The Lord is close to the brokenhearted
and saves those who are crushed in spirit
(Ps 34:18).

Home task

1. Read Ephesians 4:31–32 and Colossians 3:5–8, and jot down any of these characteristics of your earthly fallen nature that persist in showing up. Whether they are strictly emotions or not, you are told to put them to death and get rid of them. Do as Paul says. The four steps outlined under 'Handling Sinful Emotions' on page 43 will help you in doing this.

2. Emotions are powerful motivators. They move us to action. Read the first account in Scripture of sinful emotions and the action that resulted (Gen 4:1–12).

(a) What are the two emotions that moved Cain to murder his brother?

(b) God's questions to him (v.6) suggest a third emotion. What do you think it was?

(c) Do you see any similarity in the murder of Cain and the crucifixion of Christ (Mt 27:17–18)? Is there a lesson for us?

For further study

Psalms 42 and 43 were one Psalm in the original Hebrew. Study these two Psalms (only sixteen verses). You will find the writer is battling with an attack of depression. Try to find answers to the following:

(a) What do the two Psalms reveal of the causes of his depression?

46

(b) Though his sky is presently overcast, in some of the things he says shafts of sunlight break through. Pick these out, and use them to set out some spiritual remedies for being 'down in the dumps'.

A Sound Judgement

Read
1 Corinthians 4:1–5; 6:1–6.

To judge or not to judge

We have studied the renewing of the mind in general, but now we must focus on a very important function of the mind: the exercise of our judgement. It concerns the process by which we discern or evaluate, and so form opinions and make decisions. It is something we do naturally all the time. For example, I feel in urgent need of fresh air, but the weather outside is cold and it is threatening to rain. Shall I go out for a walk, or leave it till later? I decide to go. All right, shall I wear an overcoat for warmth, or a raincoat in case it rains? When I return, I shall know if my two judgements were sound!

When we come to the much more important business of judging the character or conduct of others we may find ourselves in difficulty. Should we do it at all? Sometimes the Bible seems to say 'No' and at other times 'Yes'. Since the Bible never contradicts itself, it is a challenge to look a little deeper. It usually means that the Scripture is referring to different things, as with the two passages in our reading.

What it means to judge

First, let us notice briefly a number of different ways in which the Bible refers to human judgement. Later, we will look at some of these more closely and the appropriate Bible references. There is *the judgement of condemnation*, which springs from a critical or condemning spirit. This 'playing the judge', or sitting in judgement on one another, is what Jesus told us we were *not* to do. Both our Lord and Paul taught that when we judge one another critically we are condemning ourselves, for we are guilty of the same sort of thing. What we need to do is to judge *ourselves* and bring correction to *ourselves*. Only then would we be in a position to concern ourselves with our brother's deficiencies. This is *the judgement of self-examination*.

We are often exhorted to turn away from what is evil and to imitate what is good. How can we do this unless we distinguish between the two? That calls for *the judgement of discernment*. Do you remember that we touched on this in our opening study? The ability 'to distinguish good from evil' is a very important aspect of maturing spiritually.

There is another aspect of this discerning judgement. For example, when a spiritual gift, such as prophecy, is operating in the church, we are not to accept everything that is uttered without discrimination. We are to 'weigh' and to 'test' what is said. You might call this *the judgement of evaluation*. Similarly, with a man's ministry, it needs to be 'proved' before he is publicly appointed.

The Christian's life is to be guided continually, and not just over the big decisions. Most of our guidance does not involve special prayer, and then waiting for 'a word from God'. It comes through our *judging rightly* what the will of God is through the influence of the Holy Spirit.

Finally, there is *the judgement of corrective discipline*. There are the civic authorities—the government, the judiciary and the police—who are appointed by God to judge and punish wrong doing, and decide disputes. Within the family this is the role parents have towards their children, and in the church it falls to the leaders to whom God gives the main responsibility of maintaining good order and discipline within the house of God.

Now let us look more closely at:

Judging to condemn

This is variously described in Scripture as *condemning* a brother (Lk 6:37), *looking down on* a brother (Rom 14:10), *slandering* or *speaking against* a brother (Jas 4:11). Although we are told not to do this, it is one of the most widespread and destructive sins in the professing church. Jesus said: 'Do not judge, or you too will be judged. For in the same way you judge others, you will be judged, and with the measure you use, it will be measured to you' (Mt 7:1–2). The one who spoke these strong words had been appointed by his Father as the Judge of the Universe (Jn 5:22–23). No one on earth was better qualified to sit in judement than he, but he did not do it (Jn 8:15). Get the full force of what Jesus was saying: 'You judge your brother like that, and one day I'll judge you in the same way.' James says something similar (Jas 2:12–13).

Two men on safari were attacked by a rhino. One shinned up a tree and the other dived into a great ant-heap. A few moments later, out came the man in the ant-heap. The rhino charged again, and again the man hid himself. When he came out a second time, his exasperated friend up in the tree called out, 'Get back in, you idiot!' 'Sssh,' hissed his friend putting his finger to his mouth, 'there's a sleeping lion in there!'

Don't judge your brother because you don't know all the facts, and cannot determine his motives. We must leave judging to God's time and to the One whom God has appointed (1 Cor 4:5).

Have you ever noticed that when you point that index finger of yours at your brother, you point three fingers at yourself? Notice what Romans 2:1 says about it. In the passage just considered, where Jesus told us not to judge, he went on to say that we were hypocrites if we tried to remove 'the speck of sawdust' in our brother's eye without first tackling 'the plank' in our own (Mt 7:3–5).

A hypocrite is one who pretends to be be better than he really is. If I say, 'Joe appears to be a very enthusiastic Christian, but his motives are not pure,' it is time I examined my own motives. In the first place I am putting my brother down in order to lift myself up. I want everyone to understand that I would never be so unspiritual as to have impure motives! What Jesus would say to me is, 'Enough of that spiritual humbug! Take a long hard look at your own motives. Even if others don't know what they are like, I do.' The finest antidote to this sort of judging is to engage in the judging we call self-examination.

When we pass sentence on one another in this way without being in possession of the facts, and without ability to search into another's heart, our judgements are unrighteous. They are superficial because they are based on how things appear to us. Isaiah wrote about Jesus, 'He will not judge by what he sees with his eyes, or decide by what he hears with his ears; but with righteous-ness he will judge the needy, with justice he will give decisions for the poor of the earth' (Is 11:3–4). That's why he was in a strong position to say to his own critics and detractors, 'Stop judging by mere appearances, and make a right judgment' (Jn 7:24). What then is a right judgement?

A discerning judgement

Some people think that the judging we have been considering is wrong because it is judging *people*, while discernment has only to do with *facts*. No, this has also to do with people. When we distinguish good from evil (Heb 5:14), and the truth from the false (1 Cor 10:15), we are dealing with what people do and say. To imitate what is good (3 Jn 11), and to hold to the word that is true (1 Thess 5:21) means that I must exercise a discerning judgement as I look and listen. What makes this kind of judgement different from the other is *the purpose behind it*, and the spirit and attitude with which it is exercised.

Such spiritual judgement is very important when the gifts of the Holy Spirit are operating in the church, especially gifts of inspired utterance, such as speaking in tongues, interpretation of tongues and prophecy. We need to be sure that that the utterance is inspired by the Holy Spirit, and not by the human spirit or some other spirit. There is a gift called 'the ability to distinguish between spirits' (1 Cor 12:10). Those who receive that gift may know by revelation from God what spirit is operating. But this gift, given to the few, is not to let the rest of us off the hook. We *all* need to exercise our spiritual judgement. The command to test prophecy is not only given to the leaders or to certain gifted individuals, but to Christians in general (1 Thess 5:20–21). But how do we do it?

This is too big a question to answer fully here, but there are some simple tests that we may apply. An

utterance inspired by the Holy Spirit will never con-
tradict what that same Holy Spirit has said in his word (Is
8:20). That's why it's so important to get to know your
Bible. If the utterance fails this test it is to be rejected
forthwith. If it seems to accord with Scripture, ask, does
it do the three things that prophecy is given to do (1 Cor
14:3)? It could well contain a rebuke, bring conviction of
sin and humbling before God, but that would serve to
fulfil these three purposes. But if it brings condemnation
and confusion rather than edification, there is something
wrong. Prophecy should always be Christ-centred and
draw hearts to Christ (Rev 19:10), not to the personality
of the speaker or his gift.

Finally, you should have the peace of Christ ruling in
your heart as you listen (Col 3:15), bringing the assurance that the Holy Spirit is speaking.

Judging what the will of God is

Most Christians know that the Christian life should be a
life guided by God (Rom 8:14), and that we don't have
any in-built powers of self-direction (Jer 10:23). The Old
Testament picture of this is the children of Israel
journeying to the land of Canaan, being led by God,
through a pillar of cloud by day and a pillar of fire by
night (Ex 13:21). But many of us confine this idea of
guidance to the big decisions where we call on God for a
special 'word'. However, God was not only guiding
Israel when they came to an important crossroads, but
all the time. It should be so for us. The promise of Isaiah
58:11 still stands. But most of our guidance comes
through our human judgement—*influenced by the Holy
Spirit*.

Did you memorize that verse in the previous study?
Paul says that when your mind is renewed 'you will be

able *to test and approve what God's will is*—his good, pleasing and perfect will' (Rom 12:2, italics mine). Testing and approving is an action of your judgement. Elsewhere he speaks of every thought being taken captive 'to make it obedient to Christ' (2 Cor 10:5). When that happens God is guiding us by using our own thought processes.

Psalm 25:9 in the Authorized (King James) Version says, 'The meek will he guide in judgment: and the meek will he teach his way.' It has been said that 'meek' here means that we have a preference for God's will, and that 'judgement' refers to our own judgement. In other words, God guides those who really want his will—not necessarily through a visible sign, but by swaying their judgement, in the same way that a pair of balances are swayed by a finger on one side or the other. But if you want God to do this, you must keep your hand off. If you allow the finger of self-will to interfere you are not truly meek. We must seek God for grace to be 'humble' or 'meek' (Authorized Version) and thus free the Holy Spirit to guide us continually.

Summary

What then are the keys to possessing a sound and healthy judgement? We must take great care that we do not think and speak critically of others. And when we are aware of others' faults we need to examine our own hearts and make sure that we are not seeing a reflection of something in ourselves. We must have a mind that is well instructed in the truth of God's word. And we must have a meek spirit that desires God's will only and is continually sensitive to the Holy Spirit.

Memorize

Therefore judge nothing before the appointed time;
wait till the Lord comes. He will bring to light what is
hidden in darkness and will expose the motives of
men's hearts. At that time each will receive his praise
from God (1 Cor 4:5).

Home task

1. John talks to his friend George about a mutual friend
and church member, Bill. He tells him: 'Bill's house-
group leader has reported that Bill has not shown up at
the group meeting for some weeks and that his church
attendance generally has become very irregular. I
phoned Bill to ask if we could meet for a chat, but he said
he was too busy. When I put some pointed questions to
him about his spiritual state he was very evasive. I am
sure Bill is drifting spiritually and I am really concerned
for him. Could you make contact with him, George, as
he is an old friend of yours? And could we pray together
for him?'

John has made a spiritual judgement about Bill.
Would you think he is judging righteously or unright-
eously? Record your answer in your notebook, giving
reasons and, where possible, supportive scriptures.

2. 'The spiritual man makes judgments about all
things' (1 Cor 2:15). Write down in your notebook:

(a) What is meant by 'the spiritual man'? Do all
believers qualify? (1 Cor 3:1–4; Gal 5:13—6:3).

(b) What are the things that you would need to watch to
make such a judgement? Some of them are negative—
things you would need to avoid. Others are positive—
things you would need to cultivate.

3. Put your notebook aside, and talk to your Father

about anything he has shown you that needs adjustment in the way you think and talk about others, and how you in general make judgements about things.

For further study

1. You saw the importance of *the judgement of self-examination* in connection with our tendency to judge others. Here are some other situations in which we are to examine ourselves:

(a) To make sure that we really are 'in the faith', and not self-deceived (2 Cor 13:5).

(b) Before we partake of the Lord's Supper, so that we do not eat and drink unworthily and so come under God's judgement (1 Cor 11:27–32).

(c) To make a sober assessment of ourselves and our ministry (Rom 12:3; Gal 6:1–5).

2. We mentioned that there was a place for the judgement of corrective discipline in the church.

(a) Study what Jesus said about this in the second of his two statements about the church (Mt 18:15–18).

(b) There was a serious case of immorality in the church at Corinth (1 Cor 5). Notice how the church was reacting and how, according to Paul, they should have reacted (vv.1–2). What are the reasons Paul gives for the strong action he urges them to take? Note the teaching of verses 12 and 13 on this matter of corrective discipline.

(c) See also what Paul says about the handling of disagreements among Christians and what he thinks of one believer taking another believer to court (1 Cor 6:1–8).

(d) Notice how the church in Ephesus handled evil men, false apostles in their midst (Rev 2:1–3). Do you think that the head of the church was pleased or displeased with what they had done?

A Body for the Lord

Read
1 Cor 6:12–20.

Introduction

From ancient times there have been those who taught
that everything material, including the body, is evil, and
that man needed to be set free from this 'prison house of
the soul' in order to be spiritual. This led to extremes of
self-denial and 'harsh treatment of the body' (Col 2:21–
23). In modern times the pendulum has swung the other
way, with a tendency to pander to the body and satisfy its
every demand. Men not only beautify it but glorify it,
and almost worship it. Scripture does not support either
of these attitudes, but shows us that the body is included
in the plan of salvation (Rom 8:23) and teaches us how to
honour God through our bodies.

God pronounced it very good

In the sixth and final day of creation, as his crowning
wonder, God created man. The record says, 'The Lord
God formed man from the dust of the ground' (Gen 2:7).
That's all we know about how the man received his

59

physical body. At the end God said of all that he had made, man's body included, that 'it was very good' (Gen 1:31).

Though sin came in to mar the beautiful handiwork of the Creator, it did not alter God's original purpose. Through salvation man would be restored and God's intention for him would be fulfilled. By himself becoming flesh, Jesus has for ever stamped with purity and dignity what the Bible calls 'our lowly bodies' (Phil 3:21).

When Jesus had finished this work and returned to the Father, he did not leave his body behind. On the third day he was reunited with his body, and took it, glorified in resurrection, back to heaven. He is therefore 'the firstfruits of those who have fallen asleep' in death (1 Cor 15:20). Firstfruits are followed by harvest. If Jesus' resurrection is the firstfruits, the resurrection of his saints when he comes again will be the harvest (v.23). So the body of the believer has a glorious and eternal destiny.

For the present, God wants your body to be the means by which the life of God within you is expressed to men. Looking at our reading again, there is one *major* reason why you are to honour God with your body.

You are not your own

Notice how this is emphasized:

1. 'The body is... for the Lord' (v.13)

Not primarily for us, but for him. Just as he had a physical body prepared by God in which he did the will of God on earth (Heb 10:5–7), now the only physical body he has to continue his work on earth is that of the believer.

2. 'Your body is a temple of the Holy Spirit' (v.19)

This was fulfilling a wonderful promise that Jesus had made to his disciples when speaking of the coming of the Holy Spirit. He had said, 'If anyone loves me, he will obey my teaching. My Father will love him, and we will come to him and make our home with him' (Jn 14:23). So our bodies are a dwelling place for God by his Holy Spirit.

3. 'You are not your own; you were bought at a price' (vv.19–20)

When Jesus purchased you with his blood, he purchased your body as well as your soul. You have therefore relinquished your right to yourself. If you really believe that, it must affect what you do with your body. If you know that you have been bought—and at such a price—you will want to use that body to honour the One who has bought you. How do you do it?

Honour God

1. By keeping it holy

You might think that the questions Paul poses in verses 15–16 of our reading were very strange to put to a group of believers. But these Christians lived in Corinth, a city that was not only pagan, but renowned for its immorality—much of it in connection with the Aphrodite temple where the goddess of love was worshipped. In verses 9–11 he lists the sins that were common in Corinth and reminds the believers that that is what some of them were like before they were converted.

We have seen that God has purchased our bodies for his use. But how can a holy God live in a dirty temple? The heavenly surgeon wants to use us to perform wonderful and delicate operations on the lives of others, but how can he operate with a dirty instrument (2 Tim 2:20–22)? This involves a work of cleansing (2 Cor 7:1). There is the cleansing through the blood as we confess (1 Jn 1:7,9), and there is cleansing through the word as we apply it by faith (Eph 5:26).

2. *By presenting it to him*

'I urge you, brothers,' says Paul, 'in view of God's mercy, to offer your bodies as living sacrifices, holy and pleasing to God—which is your spiritual worship' (Rom 12:1). What this means was made vivid to me by a childhood experience.

My brother and I had been dressed up in our Sunday best, kid gloves and all, as a lady and gentleman were expected. While our parents went to fetch them, we boys whiled away the time down near a stream. At length they arrived and our proud parents introduced their two little angels. We had been taught that gentlemen always take off their gloves to shake hands with a lady, so there was a palaver while fasteners were undone and kid gloves removed. Alas, the operation only served to reveal the dirtiest little hands you ever saw! The guffaws of our visitors saved the day and covered our parents' embarrassment.

When we try to offer ourselves to God without 'clean hands and a pure heart' (Ps 24:3–4), *he* certainly doesn't treat it as a joke. We must avail ourselves of the blood and the water, as we have just seen. Instead of the phrase '*offer* your bodies', the older versions have '*present* your bodies'. I prefer that, because 'present' is a bridal word. You are not to think of some terrible act of self-sacrifice, but one of loving and eager surrender, as a bride on her wedding day presents herself to her bride-groom, to be totally his. You are now to present yourself to God, place yourself at his disposal to serve him in whatever way he chooses.

By accepting it as it is

There are Christians who hold back from offering themselves to God, because of some physical blemish or deficiency, real or imaginary. 'If only I had Jack's athletic figure.' 'I really wish I could be medium height, like Sue; who wants a lanky girl?' 'Why did I have to be lumbered with such a long nose? At school they all call me Beaky.' Such thoughts are real, even it not expressed in words. How çan you honour God with your body if you are rejecting that body?

The antidote to this wrong thinking is, first, to acknowledge that God has made you the way you are. You are not his first mistake! Moses had a problem with his natural limitations at the burning bush, because he was 'slow of speech'. He wanted to back off. What did God say to him? 'Who gave man his mouth?' (Ex 4:10–11). In other words, 'Moses, I take the responsibility for your lack of fluency, and I'm still calling you to serve me. Don't try to be wiser than Me.'

The second thing is to recognize that he made you thus for a wise and wonderful purpose. You are not the result of some mindless accident. Not only what he gives, but also what he withholds are expressions of his loving wisdom. When we recognize this, we can echo the words of David:

For you created my inmost being;
    you knit me together in my mother's womb.
I praise you because I am fearfully and wonderfully made;
    your works are wonderful, I know that full well.
My frame was not hidden from you
    when I was made in the secret place.
When I was woven together in the depths of the earth...

(Ps 139:13–15)

When you can look at your body with all its blemishes and say, 'Your works are wonderful,' you are honouring God with your body.

4. By keeping it healthy

The bodies of many believers are suffering from being worked too hard, exercised too little and fed too much. That's a sure recipe for breakdown. We are not to pamper our bodies, but we are to take care of them as the temples of the Holy Spirit.

My father, who was a preacher and a writer, used to say, 'I'd rather wear out in God's service than rust out.' He died at forty-nine, while at the height of his ministry. As a young fellow with the call of God on my life, I used to pray, 'God, let me burn out for you.' Then I noticed that God called Moses through a bush that burned, and was *not* consumed (Ex 3:3). I realized that God does not call us to wear out or burn out. He wants us to wear on and burn on! That means honouring God by taking care of our bodies and keeping them fit.

'Could I borrow your motor mower?' asked Vic.

'Sure,' replied Rob, 'but take good care of it. It's new.'

It was weeks later that Ron found a dirty mower in his shed. He hardly recognized it. The underneath of the machine was caked with matted grass, the grass box was dented and the engine wouldn't start. You could hardly blame Rob for being angry. 'That may be the way he looks after his own property,' he said, 'but that mower is mine!'

I think God wants to say to some of his children, 'The body you're treating like that belongs to me. It was bought with a price. Start honouring me with it, as though you really believed it was my dwelling place.'

64

Memorize

Do you not know that your body is a temple of the Holy Spirit, who is in you, whom you have received from God? You are not your own; you were bought at a price. Therefore honour God with your body (1 Cor 6:19–20).

Home task

You read in the notes: 'If you really believe that (you have been bought with a price and belong to God) it must affect what you do with your body.' We are going to work through a little practical application of that. The first task is more particularly for God's sons and the second for his daughters.

God' sons

We have seen that we honour God by keeping our bodies healthy, and that this may be undermined by working them too hard and feeding them too much.

(a) Overwork: Write down in your notebook the reasons why people overwork. The verses in brackets will give some biblical clues to help you to fill out your answers (Prov 19:2; 1 Cor 10:14 with Col 3:5; Prov 23: 4–5 with 1 Tim 6:9). If any of these scriptures apply to you write down the practical measures you plan to take to remedy this. Then talk to God about them.

(b) Overeating: The less polite word for this is 'gluttony', which means eating greedily or excessively. Write down in your notebook why this is dishonouring to the Lord (Prov 23:19–21; Acts 24:25 with Gal 5:22–23; Rom 8:12–14; 1 Cor 9:24–27). If this is an area where

you are not in God's victory, take the same steps as outlined under (a).

God's daughters

Your task concerns honouring God by the way you clothe and adorn your body.

1. Read 1 Timothy 2:9–10 and 1 Peter 3:3–4. Put down in your notebook:

(a) All that these verses teach about how a woman of God should dress.

(b) What they say you should avoid.

(c) What is the one thing that both passages are stressing?

2. Do you think these scriptures allow a woman of God to be careless or slapdash about her appearance? Write down your answer and give reasons. You will find answers in the description of the woman of noble character in Proverbs 31:10–31. If this study has shown you the need of adjusting your own outlook and practice, decide what change is needed, write it down in your notebook and then talk to God about it.

For further study

1. Hebrews 10:22 speaks of our drawing near to God, 'having our bodies washed with pure water'. Consider the spiritual meaning of this (cf Jn 15:3; Eph 5:25–27).

2. Romans 8:11–14 promises complete victory over sin when you:

(a) Offer yourselves to God as those brought from death to life.

(b) Offer the parts of your body to God as instruments of righteousness.

Work out what that means in practical terms.

3. In Matthew 5:29–30 Jesus spoke of an eye or a

hand causing us to sin. Consider the sort of temptation he was referring to (vv.27–28) and how one would practically carry out the instruction that he gave.

Taming the Tongue

Read
James 3:1–8.

Introduction

It is the tongue that brings the message of salvation, and the tongue by which the lie of the devil is spread. By the tongue men confess Christ and by the tongue they deny him. How much comfort and encouragement, illumination and enrichment have come to men through a tongue inspired by the Holy Spirit. But how much damage has been done in the church by an unrestrained tongue. It has 'the power of life and death' (Prov 18:21). A mature Christian is one who has every part of his being, especially his tongue, under the rule of Christ.

The power of the tongue

In our reading the tongue is likened to the bit in the horses' mouth and to the rudder of a great ship (vv.3–4). Each is small in size but great in influence. He who controls the bit controls the horse, and he who controls the rudder steers the ship. Even so, he who controls his tongue is able to bridle his whole body (v.2). This is not said of any other part of the body. Why does this small member play such a key role?

In Study 3 (The Mind Renewed) we learned that the way you think in your heart reveals your true character. So God never assesses us by outward appearance but what we are in our hearts (1 Sam 16:7). It is the heart that controls the tongue. 'Out of the overflow of the heart the mouth speaks' (Mt 12:34).

> The tongue also is a fire, a world of evil among the parts of the body. It corrupts the whole person, sets the whole course of his life on fire, and is itself set on fire by hell...no man can tame the tongue. It is a restless evil, full of deadly poison (vv.6, 8).

That's the human tongue—apart from the grace of God. Why such strong language? Because Scripture and experience teach us how totally corrupt is the human heart (Jer 17:9). It is because the heart is incurable that the tongue is untamable. But 'what is impossible with men is possible with God' (Lk 18:27). The One who can change our sinful hearts (and has he not begun this miraculous work?) can by the same means bring the unruly member under control.

We shall now look at four important areas where this needs to happen.

A lying tongue

With lying there must be *the intention to deceive*. To speak what is incorrect is not lying if the speaker believes it to be true. Satan is both 'the father of lies' (Jn 8:44) and 'the deceiver of the whole world' (Rev 12:9, RSV). 'Do not lie to each other,' says Paul, 'since you have taken off your old self with its practices and have put on the new self, which is being renewed in knowledge in the image of its Creator' (Col 3:9–10). To do so is to sin against the body, for we are all fellow members of that one body (Eph 4:25). Loving and practising any form of falsehood is the characteristic of those whose final destiny is exclusion for ever from the City of God (Rev 22:15).

Worldly people may disapprove of 'black lies' but justify 'white lies', when they deem the motive of the untruth to be good. For example, a doctor may lie to a patient who is terminally ill with cancer, because he doesn't want to upset his patient. The fact is that every person, believer or unbeliever, has a right to know that he is approaching the great terminus of life, where all passengers have to change. He may need to make his peace with God, or put things right with his fellow men. No, all lies are black.

Perhaps you never tell a barefaced lie, but are there *grey areas* where you skirt the truth?

'What is the purpose of your visit to the USA?' asked the immigration officer. I had been warned that to say I had come to preach could lead to further questions about payments for preaching, and create difficulties. I was advised: 'Just say that you are visiting friends.' This was true, but was not 'the truth' for it would have misled the officer. I told him the truth, and the warning proved true. I did get asked further questions, but in five minutes I was through—with a clear conscience.

Another grey area is *exaggeration*. Pride is normally the motive. We want to impress, and the plain unvarnished truth is not all that impressive so we enlarge, embellish and fill in imaginary details from the storehouse of our own wishful thinking. This is a form of 'unwholesome talk' which grieves the Holy Spirit (Eph 4:29–30). One kind of exaggeration that smacks of insincerity and hypocrisy is *flattery*, or false praise. It is buttering someone up for our own advantage (Jude 16). Scripture equates this kind of speech with lying (Prov 26:28). Because it is something that God hates (Job 32:22) we must hate it too.

A backbiting tongue

Backbiting, gossipping and criticizing are forms of evil speaking which have wrought terrible havoc in the church of Jesus Christ. The devil is the father of this activity also. 'A whisperer separates close friends' (Prov 16:28, RSV), and in the Garden Satan whispered things in the heart of Eve, which blackened God's good character, and resulted in the break up of a beautiful friendship between God and man (Gen 3:4–5).

We noticed in Study 5 (A Sound Judgement) that speech which puts others down is designed to exalt the speaker. Often there is a spirit of jealousy and competitiveness behind it. Miriam and Aaron criticized Moses for marrying a Cushite wife but they were simply jealous of Moses' position (Num 12:1–2). We see the humility of Moses in his refusal to defend himself (v.3) and how God showed his anger when he intervened to defend his servant (v.9). It is specially grevious to God when there is this kind of criticism against his appointed leaders. He says, 'Do not touch my anointed ones; do my prophets no harm' (Ps 105:15).

Persistent backbiting and criticism had broken the spirit of a servant of God. When he became gravely ill one of the chief culprits became conscience-stricken and went to him to confess and ask forgiveness. 'I forgive you, but I want you to take this pillow to the window and shake out the feathers,' said the sick man. He did so. 'Now go collect up the feathers,' was the next request. 'That I cannot do,' was the reply. 'Nor can you undo the false things you have said about me,' replied the other;

'they will be put right at the judgment seat of Christ' (2 Cor 5:10; Col 3:25).

A grumbling tongue

From the moment God's people were redeemed they began to grumble. Whenever they were discontented with their lot they looked for a scapegoat. Usually they picked on Moses and Aaron. So often grumbling among God's people is directed against leaders. This is not to say that leaders never make mistakes. If they do, there are ways to rectify the situation, but grumbling is not one of them. In fact, Moses pointed out that the Israelites were really grumbling against God (Ex 16:8). They were rebelling against his ordering of their lives. We read of God's anger being aroused when he heard them complaining (Num 11:1). What do you think he feels when he hears our grumbling?

Perhaps we may feel that Paul and Silas had an excuse for complaining, when in the midst of their campaign in Philippi they were wrongfully arrested, beaten and flung into prison. No prospect of any sleep at that midnight hour with their backs bleeding and their feet fastened in the stocks. But read what they did, and then what God did in response (Acts 16:25–30). That is the way to face situations that seem to go wrong.

A talkative tongue

There is a time to be silent as well as a time to speak (Eccles 3:7). Some believers are silent when they should speak, some speak when they should be silent, and others seem to talk all the time.

A wife was suing for divorce on the grounds that her husband hadn't spoken to her in years. 'Is that really true?' asked the incredulous judge. 'Well, 'er,' replied the husband, 'I, 'er just didn't like to interrupt!'

We are told that 'a chattering fool comes to ruin' (Prov 10:8), but that 'a man of knowledge uses words with restraint' (Prov 17:27). Similarly the New Testament warns us to 'avoid godless chatter' (2 Tim 2:16). Why is this so important? Firstly, self-control which is one segment of the fruit of the Spirit (Gal 5:23), is essential in every aspect of our lives, but especially in our speech. In a great flow of words we can boast, exaggerate, misrepresent, confuse and, before we realize it, say things that we may later regret. 'When words are many, sin is not absent' (Prov 10:19).

The New Testament is equally clear: 'Everyone should be quick to listen, slow to speak and slow to become angry' (Jas 1:19). If an unrestrained and undisciplined tongue exposes you to the temptation of the devil, it is equally true that by guarding your lips you guard your soul (Prov 13:3).

How to tame it

1. *You must be convinced that it can be tamed*

This is by the grace of God. 'No *man* can tame the tongue' means that you are closed off to Christ. Read about the power that enables him to bring everything under his control (Phil 3:21). A few verses later comes that tremendous confession, 'I can do everything through [Christ] who gives me strength' (4:13). Make that confession your very own. Confess it until you fully believe it. What follows will only be effective if you hold fast to this confession.

2. *Acknowledge where it needs to be tamed*

Wherever the Holy Spirit has brought conviction you need to acknowledge that to God. In fact, we have only

dealt with four of the more common sins of the tongue.
There are many others. God may want to put his finger
on speech that is unwholesome (i.e. unclean or
suggestive), boastful, unkind, bitter, derisive or
whatever. What the Holy Spirit pinpoints take to God in
humble confession.

3. Bring every area of failure under the rule of Christ

'Lord, I have confessed that power which enables you to
bring everything under your control. I now hand over
my tongue to you. Take control over it. Subdue those
words that are critical, unkind [or whatever the Holy
Spirit has brought to your attention]. So cleanse my
heart that I will not even want to speak such words.
Make my lips instead to show forth your praise. Amen.'

Memorize

Set a guard over my mouth, O Lord;
Keep watch over the door of my lips.
(Ps 141:3)

Home task

1. Under 'How to tame it' above, go through the three
steps with your notebook. *In the first place* ask yourself
whether you really believe that your tongue can be
tamed. Meditate on Philippians 3:21; 4:13 and John
8:36, until with real conviction you can write in your
notebook, 'I believe that this tongue of mine can be
brought under Christ's rule.'

Secondly, pinpoint by confession to God the sins of
the tongue that you know you need to deal with. Don't
be discouraged if you feel, 'I sin so much here I don't
know where to begin.' Let the Holy Spirit focus on those

that he sees are urgent. Write them down in your notebook.

Finally, use the prayer suggested—or better still, one of your own—to bring each area of failure under Christ's rule. Believe he is responding as you pray. Thank him for doing so. As he shows you other areas, tackle them in the same way.

2. Now look at a tongue that was always under perfect control—that of our Lord Jesus. Notice the impression created by his first public utterance (Lk 4:22). 'Gracious words' fulfilled a prophecy made about him hundreds of years earlier (Ps 45:2). However, we are not to put him on a pedestal; rather we are to imitate him (Col 4:6). If our conversation is to be 'always full of grace' write down what that means. List first the kind of language we would need to avoid, and then the kind we would need to cultivate. Claim the promise of 2 Corinthians 12:9.

For further study

1. As we become more knowledgeable as Christians there is the temptation to become quarrelsome and argumentative. In our witnessing we can win the argument and lose the man. But Paul strongly discourages argumentativeness, especially among Christians (Phil 2:14; 1 Tim 1:4; 2:8; 6:4–5; 2 Tim 2:14, 23–25). It could disqualify a man from being an elder (1 Tim 3:3). List the reasons why we need to avoid this. What do you think lies behind an argumentative spirit?

2. Read Matthew 12:33–37. Why did Jesus teach that men would be acquitted or condemned on the day of judgement on the basis of their words? He also said that we would be held accountable for 'every careless [idle, ineffective, worthless] word'. What words would come into this category?

SECTION 2

Growing Strong

Knowing the Fear of the Lord

Read
Isaiah 8:11–17.

What is the fear of the Lord?

We must distinguish three kinds of fear in human
experience.

Natural fear

For example, reacting to a situation of physical danger.
Driving home one winter's day, I was travelling too fast
for the icy road conditions. The car began to swing to the
wrong side just as another car appeared, coming towards
me. Gripped with the fear of a head-on smash I wrestled
to correct the skid. Still out of control, it swung back as
the approaching car shot past. This instinctive fear which
we have all felt—the fear that motivates us to act to
preserve our lives—is not sinful, it is natural.

Sinful fear

This may prevent us from doing the will of God, for
example, not owning up to some wrong doing; or compel
us to do what is not God's will, like Peter denying the
Lord. This may come as a sudden attack, as with Elijah

(1 Kings 19:1–4), or it may be an habitual thing, a slavery of the devil to a certain kind of fear (Heb 2:15). How prone we are to fear is apparent from the fact that there are 366 occasions in the Bible where God tells us, 'Fear not.'

Godly fear, or the fear of the Lord

The fact that Scripture sometimes links this kind of fear with trembling (Phil 2:12) proves that we are talking about the same basic human emotion as the other two. Modern translations that replace the word 'fear' with 'reverance' or 'respect' are weakening it. There is a good reason why the Holy Spirit, with many alternatives at his disposal, has used the word 'fear' in both the Old and New Testaments. If the emotion is the same with the three different kinds of fear, the source and the motivation are very different with godly fear.

The fear of the Lord depends on a right understanding of God's character. You could have a wrong view of God, thinking him to be unjust, unmerciful or even tyrannical, and that might make you frightened of him. That would be sinful fear, *not* the fear of the Lord (see Lk 19:21). Sinful fear is always self-centred, while godly fear is always God-centred.

Why do we need it?

Scriptures on this neglected theme are so numerous, especially in the Old Testament, that we shall only be able to touch on the more important aspects. The fear of the Lord is one of the great motivating factors of the Christian life. It is a corrective when we are tempted to deviate from the centre of God's will and follow some by-path meadow, and it is an antidote to so much that may be dubbed 'Christian', but which is shallow and superficial. It will ensure:

1. A right attitude to God

There was a holy intimacy with God that marked the lives of men like Abraham (Jas 2:23) and Moses (Deut 34:10). That is something we should all seek. But there is a wrong kind of familiarity that addresses this awesome and majestic God as though he were one of our buddies, and that tries to bring him down to our level. What is lacking here is godly fear. None of us will ever attain to God's friendship unless we retain a sense of awe and wonder in our approach. This will affect us in all our dealings with him. It will make our worship acceptable because we recognize that 'our God [not just the God of the unbeliever] is a consuming fire' (Heb 12:28–29).

2. A needful repugnance for sin

'To fear the Lord is to hate evil' (Prov 8:13). Sin is repugnant to us. We may occasionally be deceived by the enemy, or tempted by the devil, but we will never flirt with sin. If we are tripped and fall into the mire, we will never wallow in it. Instead we respond in the words of Micah 7:8 as we pick ourselves up. The fear of the Lord will cause us to take avoiding action when we see sin looming ahead (Prov 16:6). There are particular temptations that are defeated by showing the enemy a clean pair of heels (1 Cor 6:18; 10:14; 2 Tim 2:22).

3. A prayer life that prevails

You will find that the great recorded prayers of the Bible were saturated with the fear of God, especially those offered for the restoration of God's people and of God's house. See how Daniel addresses God (Dan 9:4), and the true humility that characterized his praying (v.7). We sense the same tone with the praying of our Lord,

'Father...Holy Father...O righteous Father' (Jn 17:1, 11, 25). We are told, 'In the days of his flesh, Jesus offered up prayers and supplications, with loud cries and tears, to him who was able to save him from death, and *he was heard for his godly fear*' (Heb 5:7, RSV, italics mine). Notice that Jesus didn't get any head start in prayer because he was God's Son. He prevailed because he prayed with a true appreciation of God's character. If we have godly fear we shall also prevail.

4. A pure motivation for service

As Christians we don't need to be told more things to do. We have been exhorted to do so much, and the list gets longer with every message we hear, or every Bible study we go through. We need to be *motivated* to start doing the things we know to do. There is no more effective motivation for service than the fear of God. Fearing the Lord and serving him go together in Scripture (Deut 6:13; 10:12; Josh 24:14). Onlookers must have thought Noah's building of the ark was crazy, but the motivation for his obedience was 'holy fear' (Heb 11:7). Do you find reluctance to speak to people about Christ? Paul knew that too, but note what it was that overcame his reluctance (2 Cor 5:11).

5. A means to make holiness perfect

Says Paul, 'Let us cleanse ourselves from every defilement of body and spirit, and make holiness perfect in the fear of God' (2 Cor 7:1, RSV). To make holiness perfect does not mean to reach sinless perfection (1 Jn 1:8–10). Only Jesus ever lived on earth a completely sinless life (1 Pet 2:22). It means 'perfect' in the sense of coming to full growth or maturity. This would mean that we live in Christ's promised victory, display the fruit of the Spirit (Gal 5:22–23), and that failure is the exception rather than the rule. Cleansing ourselves is the negative side of perfecting holiness, becoming like Jesus in our character is the positive. Why do we need the fear of the Lord? It creates within us a longing to be God-like, and it provides within us the motivation and faith to make it happen.

6. A release from sinful fear

'Do not call conspiracy everything that these people call conspiracy; do not fear what they fear, and do not dread it. The Lord Almighty...he is the one you are to fear' (Is 8:12–13). Are we gripped by the fears that haunt the world—fear of sickness, of unemployment, of violence, of nuclear war, etc? Only if the fear of the Lord has not taken over.

A member of a bomber crew whose plane has been hit and set on fire may be fearful at the thought of ejecting and committing himself to his parachute. But he does so because of the greater fear of staying in a blazing plane. The greater fear overcomes the lesser.

It was a fearful thing for Abraham to raise the knife to slay his son. But the moment he did God stayed his hand saying, 'Now I know that *you fear God*' (Gen 22:12). An epitaph to Sir John Lawrence of India in Westminster Abbey says, 'He feared man so little because he feared God so much.' There is no antidote to the fears that plague the human heart as effective as the fear of the Lord.

How do you get it?

The fear of God and the knowledge of God go together (Prov 2:5). It was said of the coming Messiah, 'The Spirit of the Lord will rest on him...the Spirit of knowledge and of the fear of the Lord—and he will delight in the fear of the Lord' (Is 11:2–3). Notice that there was nothing fearsome about this fear. Jesus didn't have to steel himself to practice it. He delighted in it, and so shall we. This passage shows us that it is the work of the Spirit, and that it is linked with knowledge. What kind of knowledge does the Holy Spirit bring?

First and foremost the knowlege of God. This is the revelation of God that Paul prayed the Ephesian church might have (Eph 1:17). The more we have of this the more we shall know of the fear of the Lord.

This work of the Holy Spirit doesn't happen automatically, or we wouldn't need to be answering this question. Those who experience the fear of the Lord are those who desire it deeply. It is a result of seeking the Lord—not just praying. There is a difference (2 Chron 7:14). When you pray you expect to get answers. When you seek God you expect to make a new discovery. Read Jeremiah 29:11–13. Verse 13 gives the key:

It tells me that I will seek God and find him. When I seek him _____

Memorize

Continue to work out your salvation with fear and trembling, for it is God who works in you to will and to act according to his good pleasure (Phil 2:12–13).

Home task

1. Ephesians 6:5 says, 'Slaves, obey your earthly masters with respect and fear, and with sincerity of heart, just as you would obey Christ.' This applies equally to the employer/employee relationship today. The fear is not primarily fear of the boss, but the fear of the Lord (cf Col 3:22 'fearing the Lord'). List the kinds

of things that a Christian employee, with the fear of the Lord in his heart, might do that others would probably not do, and that he would not do that others probably would. Is this an attitude you need only adopt if the boss is nice (1 Pet 2:18)?

2. The fear of the Lord is not only to characterize the individual believer, but the whole church. In the first reference in Scripture to 'the house of God' (Gen 28:16–17), note down what it says about Jacob (v.17). Then turn to Acts 9:31. Write down what you think would be the difference between a church 'living in the fear of the Lord', and one that was not.

For further study

Read Philippians 2:12–13. Paul says 'work out your salvation'. Write down:

1. What you think Paul meant by this, in practical terms.

2. Where you think the Philippian Christians were failing to do this. The following references will give you some clues (1:27; 2:2–4, 14–15; 4:2).

3. Why he says that they were to do it 'with fear and trembling'. How would this influence the spiritual problem considered in question 2?

Finding God's Will

Read

Colossians 1:9–14.

Introduction

We have touched on one aspect of this theme in Study 5 (A Sound Judgement). It would be good to re-read the section 'Judging what the will of God is'. But Spirit-directed judgement is only one way in which we come to know God's will. The whole theme is one of paramount importance. We saw in that earlier study that we don't have any inbuilt powers of self-direction (Jer 10:23). We need to be guided by God—especially over important decisions, such as career, life partner, what church to join, where to live, the friends we make. Then we need to know God's will on many other wider issues. It concerns the whole way God wants us to live and behave, work and witness. This is essential to our becoming mature. See how Epaphras prayed for his fellow Christians (Col 4:12).

Think first of relationship

Knowing God's will is so much more than learning some technique of guidance, or applying certain principles.

87

We need to think less about method and more about relationship. I had been ministering at a church in a distant city. Before leaving I asked one of the leaders if he could put me on the right road for my return journey. I was expecting instructions, but he gave me a guide. 'Neil will pilot you. He takes that route home anyway.' Instead of trying to decipher some scribbled directions as I drove, I had only to keep in touch with Neil in the blue Datsun.

God didn't give the Israelites a route to follow. He himself went ahead of them to guide them on their way (Ex 13:21).

Whether it is guidance in specific decisions or just understanding the will of God in important matters of life, relationship is the key. If we are living in disobedience and therefore out of touch with God we cannot expect to receive God's guidance, even though we may pray earnestly for it (1 Sam 28:5–6, 15; Ps 66:18–19). We must be in right relationship with the Guide.

Learn from Paul's prayer

Paul's prayer in our reading confirms what we have been saying.

> We have not stopped...asking God to fill you with the knowledge of his will through all spiritual wisdom and understanding...that you may live a life worthy of the Lord and may please him in every way: bearing fruit in every good work, growing in the knowledge of God.

Note:

For whom Paul prays

Not simply for the leaders of the church, but for *all* the believers. Paul could pray like this with confidence, because when he was newly converted he was told that God had chosen him 'to know his will' (Acts 22:14). You too have been chosen to know God's will.

For what Paul prays

Not simply that the Colossians may be informed as to what the will of God is, but to be *filled* with the knowledge of it. To be filled with the Spirit is to be possessed and ruled by the Spirit. To be filled with the knowledge of God's will means that you are so ruled by that will that you carry it out. That's what Paul wanted for the Colossians, and that's what God wants for us.

With these results, we are firstly to *'live a life worthy of the Lord'*. How can we live such a life if we have never troubled to find out what pleases and what displeases God, or what his particular will is for our lives?

Secondly, *'bearing fruit in every good work'*. If we know the will of God and are doing it by the power of the Holy Spirit we cannot help being fruitful.

Lastly, and most wonderful of all, *'growing in the knowledge of God'*. This means that the relationship with our divine Guide that we spoke about earlier is continually deepening. Knowing God's will and knowing God are closely related.

A young man was trying to persuade his friend to go with him to a certain questionable establishment in town.

'No thanks,' said the other.

'Why not?'

'It would upset my dad,'

'Oh I see. He's told you not to go there?'

'No, he hasn't—but I know my dad.'

Not only is it true—getting to know God's will you get to know God, but getting to know God you get to know his will, especially over many 'Is it right?—Is it wrong?' issues.

Importance of heart attitude

If anyone finds the business of ascertaining God's will difficult, it is usually because the heart attitude is not right. Here are four requirements:

1. Dependence

Any sense of self-sufficiency must be broken down if we are to trust God with all our heart and not lean on our own understanding (Prov 3:5–6). Common sense and human wisdom will prove totally inadequate. We are required to understand what the will of the Lord is. Not to do so is 'foolish' (Eph 5:17). We will not discover God's will by trying to fathom it with our human intellect (Job 11:7), but by God revealing it in answer to prayer (Eph 1:17–19).

2. Obedience

This is never a problem—till you discover that God's will crosses yours! After the fall of Jerusalem to the Babylonians, the leaders of the Israelites who were not carried away into captivity asked the prophet Jeremiah to enquire from God where they should go and what they should do. God was their witness that they would do whatever the Lord said (Jer 42:1–6). But see how they responded when God did speak (Jer 43:1–2). More often than not God will not trouble to reveal his will to us if we are not disposed to obey it. Jesus once said that his teaching was not his own but God's, and that if anyone chose to do God's will they would know that this was the case (Jn 7:16–17). In the same way, if we have hearts truly set to do God's will, we shall know assuredly what God's will is.

90

3. Patience

When we enquire of the Lord it is not often we get a
reply by return of post. This is where our determination
to obey is put to the test. We must learn to wait for God.
While we wait he is acting for us (Is 64:4). How often
Christians ask God for direction, and when he doesn't
answer as quickly as they would like they do whatever
they think best. That is, they 'lean on [their] understanding' (see above). Often God's zero hour is just after
ours. We must wait for God. Failure to do this was King
Saul's first major blunder, and it cost him his throne (1
Sam 13:7–14). If our hearts are right God will always
guide in time.

4. Sensitivity

One of the great Bible promises for knowing God's will
is Psalm 32:8–9. Instead of 'I will counsel you and watch
over you' most versions read, 'I will counsel you with my
eye upon you.' The eye is a very sensitive but effective
method of counselling. I recall occasions when we had
visitors to tea, and my brother and I were tucking into
the cream cakes before anyone else had a look in—until
we caught Father's eye! That was enough. No words
were needed.

As Christians that means keeping our eye on the Lord
to pick up the signals, just as one serving at table would
watch the master or mistress (Ps 123:1–2). After
promising to counsel us with his eye (Ps 32:8), the Lord
tells us, 'Do not be like the horse or the mule.' Does God
have to tug you first this way and then that to get you
where he wants you? That's the only way he can deal
with some. Pray for sensitivity to those gentle checks or
nudges of the Holy Spirit.

How God communicates

Finally we must consider briefly the practical ways by which God communicates his will to us. First, there are the *Scriptures*. As well as using these in general to teach us, God often lights up a phrase or passage to give us special direction.

When I received my first invitation to minister God's word overseas there seemed no way that I could say 'Yes'. Then this scripture came strongly to me, 'Go; I will help you speak and will teach you what to say' (Ex 4:12). I took it as God's word, and amazingly the obstacles were removed one by one.

Then there is the *inward voice* of the Holy Spirit (Acts 10:19–20). We often read of God speaking to the Old Testament saints, but seldom it would seem with an audible voice; rather with that 'still small voice' within. We have the inward sensing that we have heard from God.

There is also the *ordering of our circumstances*. God has a way of cutting off finance and of releasing it; of shutting doors and opening them (1 Cor 16:8–9), and he uses these to move us, or keep us where we are.

We must include here the *counsel of others*, especially our leaders. We are not loners serving God. We are members that belong to each other and have a concern for each other in the body of Christ (1 Cor 12:25–26). It should not surprise us that God may give or confirm his direction to us through fellow-members of the body.

God also uses *the gifts of the Holy Spirit*. The first missionary movement was set in motion by a direct word from the Holy Spirit, probably through one of the prophets present (Acts 13:1–3). Note that this word was a confirmation, setting two men apart for the work to which God had already called them. If such an utterance is not a confirmation, it will need to be tested and confirmed (1 Thess 5:20–21). God may also use *dreams*, as in Bible times, to enlighten us, warn us, or give us special direction (Mt 2:12–13).

Invariably God uses two or more means in a given situation to communicate his will. If you are not sure, stay put until you are. There is one final indication that should be present every time you think you discern the will of God—*the peace of God* ruling in your heart (Col 3:15). The word 'rule' here means to arbitrate, or act as referee. When your peace is disturbed, the referee has blown his whistle to stop the game. Never move if the peace of God is not ruling in your heart.

Memorize

I will instruct you and teach you in the way you should go; I will counsel you and watch over you. Do not be like the horse or the mule, which have no understanding but must be controlled by bit and bridle or they will not come to you (Ps 32:8–9).

Home task

1. Write in your notebook your honest answer to the following personal questions. Write out in full any scripture with its reference that confirms your answer.
(a) Do you believe that God has a plan for your future which is good, well-pleasing and perfect?
(b) Are you expecting him to unfold, or to continue to unfold, that plan to you?
(c) Are you willing to forego any plan of yours if it should clash with God's revealed plan?
(d) For you to know God's will, God has his part to play and you have yours. What is your part?

For further study

1. Study the track record of Saul over this question of seeking God's will (often called 'enquiring of the Lord'), and then that of David. Write down all you can learn from these incidents of the characters of these two men.

Saul: 1 Samuel 14:16–20 (the ark was used for consulting God); 36–37; 28:6; 1 Chronicles 10:13–14; 13:3.

David: 1 Samuel 23:2, 4; 30:8; 2 Samuel 2:1; 5:19, 23; 21:1.

2. Isaiah 30:21 is a promise that if we mistake God's path for us he will correct us. The voice *behind us* tells us our Shepherd is no longer leading us, and turning to right or left means deviating from the right path (Num 20:17; Deut 5:32). See what you can learn from two examples of God's corrective guidance in the life of David, and two from the life of Paul:

David: 1 Samuel 25:1–34; 2 Samuel 7:1–16.
Paul: Acts 16:6–7.

Resisting the Tempter

Read
1 Peter 5:5–11.

Who is the tempter?

Satan was a very high angelic dignitary, one of the cherubim, until he and his angels rebelled and were expelled from heaven (Is 14:12–14; Ezek 28:14–16). It is these powers of darkness, not human beings, who are now our real enemy (Eph 6:12). Satan (meaning adversary) is committed to opposing God and all those who belong to God's kingdom.

Satan's objective

Since his ambition was to make himself 'like the Most High' (Is 14:14) he sought to tempt that first pair to transfer their allegiance to him. He first seduced Eve into disobeying God, then through her Adam (Gen 3:1–6). The attack was on Eve's mind, and Satan came in the guise of a serpent, which suggests cunning and deceit (2 Cor 11:3). In this way he succeeded in injecting the germ of rebellion into the human race, so that death came on all (Rom 5:12). The measure of Satan's success is that he is acknowledged in Scripture as 'the prince of this world' (Jn 12:31) and 'the god of this age' (2 Cor 4:4). He has 'blinded the minds of unbelievers' to keep them from seeing the light and knowing who it is they are serving. Now 'the whole world is under the control of the evil one' (1 Jn 5:19).

God's intervention

Now for the bright side. Satan's success caused no panic in heaven. Nothing took God by surprise. His plan of salvation was prepared before the need for it came into existence (Rev 13:8). The coming of Jesus was like D-day in Europe, a strategic attack by the kingdom of heaven to recapture lost territory. His preaching the kingdom, healing the sick and casting out demons was stage one of this heavenly invasion (Mt 12:28). Stage two was to be accomplished through that army of redeemed men and women called the church, formed at Pentecost. And the final victory will be when the last trumpet sounds heralding Christ's return in glory, and a mighty cry is heard from heaven: 'The kingdom of the world has become the kingdom of our Lord and of his Christ, and he will reign for ever and ever' (Rev 11:15). Not only does the believer have the assurance of ultimate victory, but even Satan himself knows that his days are numbered (Rev 12:12).

Don't underestimate your enemy...

This is a common mistake of believers. They think that 'the roaring lion' is toothless, all bark and no bite. Or they think that deception is his only weapon, that he can only pull the wool over your eyes. We must take the devil seriously. He is a spirit being with supernatural power. He brought down fire from the sky and a storm from the desert that dealt death and destruction to Job's household and possessions (Job 1:12, 16, 18–19). He was able to transport the Son of God from the desert and set him on the highest point of the temple in Jerusalem (Mt 4:5). Then from a high place he was able to show him all the kingdoms of the world in the flash of a second (Lk 4:5). If we have the fear of the Lord we shall maintain a healthy respect for the authority God has given Satan. If the great archangel was not free to slander him, we must be careful how we speak about him or address him (Jude 8—9).

... but don't see him too big

It is just as serious a mistake to think that Satan has a free hand to do what he wants. Far from it. Since 'the world, and all who live in it' belong to the Lord (Ps 24:1), the devil is God's devil, and owes his existence and authority to the Most High. He is only 'ruler of the world' and 'God of this age' by divine permission, and until God decides to settle accounts (Rev 20:10). He cannot lift a little finger against God's children without God's approval. He launched two fierce attacks on Job, but observe how they were monitored and controlled by God (Job 1:12; 2:6), and permitted for Job's ultimate good and blessing (Job 42:12; Jas 5:11). Our temptations too are controlled by God (1 Cor 10:13).

God meant it for good

Though God may lead us into temptation (Mt 4:1; Acts 20:22–23), or permit us to be tempted, he himself never tempts us to do evil (Jas 1:13). If God can control our temptations we may wonder why he doesn't intervene to stop them altogether. It is because they accomplish a valuable purpose in our lives. What is God doing through temptation?

1. Strengthening your faith by putting it to the test

Faith is like muscle. The athlete is subjected to greater and greater tests in order to reach his peak performance. Strong winds that cause the trees to bend also drive their roots deeper into the soil. Without temptation faith would be flabby (Jas 1:2–4; 1 Pet 1:6–7).

2. Purifying your character as gold in a crucible

Before he went through the fire of trial Job was *'righteous'*. That had more to do with his outward acts. *After* the fire Job was *holy*, for God had dealt with inner attitudes. He had said himself, 'When he has tested me, I shall come forth as gold' (Job 23:10).

3. Maturing you for God's approval

It is only having 'stood the test' under trial that we qualify for 'the crown of life' (Jas 1:12).

Two pocket watches in a jeweller's appeared to be absolutely identical except that one was twice the price of the other. The reason? The more expensive one had undergone stringent tests, such as being subjected to enormous pressure, great extremes of temperature, immersed in water for days, and suchlike, and had come through unaffected. But God intends that we shall not ony come through unscathed, but made 'strong, firm and steadfast' (1 Pet 5:10).

An old Puritan was watching a blacksmith tempering metal. With the rod in his hand he pointed to different parts of the red-hot iron, and wherever he pointed, his assistant brought down the sledge hammer with a great thud. The Puritan saw how God points out where we need tempering, and there the devil brings down the hammer of temptation. 'Thus I perceived,' he said, 'how God makes the devil sweat for the saints' good!' The devil meant it for harm, but God meant it for good.

How to resist

1. Take a positive attitude

This means believing what has just been said about temptation: that God means it for good.

I was lying immobilized on a hospital bed 12,000 miles from home. An accident had terminated my preaching tour in that country before I had fulfilled the main engagements I had come for. It seemed that every bone in my body was aching, as well as my injured head. And the verse God gave me was James 1:2! How do you respond to a word like that? Only by declaring in faith there and then, 'Great good will come out of this.' And, of course, it did.

Have you shuddered when you read the catalogue of Paul's hardships? He could refer to them as 'light and momentary troubles' only because he saw them in the light of what they would achieve (2 Cor 4:17–18).

2. Recognize the attack

That means being constantly alert. Jesus told a bunch of drowsy disciples, 'Watch and pray so that you will not fall into temptation' (Mt 26:41). How would you behave if you were in the bush, and you knew that there was a lion prowling around? Well, that's exactly the situation you are in, and Peter gives you the answer (1 Pet 5:8). To be proud or cocksure of ourselves is to be riding for a fall (1 Cor 10:12). Often the enemy disguises his attack. We may not be aware that that strange bout of depression or

that feeling of deep discouragement could be an attack
of the devil. Let us trust the Holy Spirit to alert us.

3. Don't court temptation or walk into danger

We are *not* to 'think about how to gratify the desires of
the sinful nature' (Rom 13:14b). The world about us will
provide endless scope for this, but the grace of God
teaches us to say 'No' (Tit 2:11–12). The sinful nature is
to be crucified, not pampered and nourished (Gal 5:24).
There are certain 'no go' areas where the child of God
trespasses at his peril. We are to have nothing to do with
anything occult, however harmless it may seem.
Spiritism (usually called spiritualism), witchcraft,
fortune-telling, horoscopes, ouija board and suchlike
are forbidden because powers of evil are operating there
(Deut 18:9–13). Any soldier who strolls into enemy
territory is liable to be taken prisoner (Acts 8:9–11,
18–23).

4. Submit to God—resist the devil (Jas 4:7)

If you do not first submit to God you have no power to
resist the devil. Submission brings God's power to your
aid. How do you resist? Not by taking a deep breath and
gritting your teeth. Our fight is one of faith (1 Tim 6:12).
So Peter tells us how to resist the roaring lion—'by
standing firm in the faith' (1 Pet 5:9). It is not even
enough to think about God's superior strength or his
promise to deliver you, you must give voice to your faith.
Confess with your mouth what you are believing in your
heart. If you memorize some of the great victory
promises you will be able to quote them in the heat of the
battle. For example:

Sin shall not be your master (Rom 6:14).

Thanks be to God! He gives us the victory through our Lord Jesus Christ (1 Cor 15:57).

We are more than conquerors through him who loved us (Rom 8:37).

Those temptations that come from within, rather than the outside attacks of the devil, will be dealt with in our next study.

Memorize

Consider it pure joy, my brothers, whenever you face trials of many kinds, because you know that the testing of your faith develops perseverance. Perseverance must finish its work so that you may be mature and complete, not lacking in anything (Jas 1:2–4).

Home task

1. Temptation is a learning time. Look back over your own experience of temptation. Note down what you have learned:
(a) about yourself
(b) about God and his word
(c) about your need of fellow Christians.
   2. Now make a note of what you believe temptation has done in making you a better Christian. Thank God for each thing you write down. And if you are still going through some temptation, start thanking God for this and confessing that you believe his purpose in it will be fulfilled, and that he is giving you the victory.

Further study

1. Jesus referred to the devil when he said, 'The thief comes only to steal and kill and destroy' (Jn 10:10). In what ways is this generally true of mankind? And in what ways does he try to rob the believer? How are we to guard against this?

2. Jesus also referred to the devil as 'a strong man' guarding the valuables in his house (Mt 12:29; Lk 11:21–22). What is his house? What are these valuables? How in practical terms are we to enter his house, tie him up and make off with his goods? Find scriptures to support your answer.

Embracing the Cross

Read
Romans 6:1–14.

Salvation past, present and future

The Bible teaches that through the cross the believer *has been saved* from the *penalty* of sin (Jn 5:24), that he *is being saved* from the *power* of sin (Rom 5:10) and one day, when Christ returns, he *will be saved* from the *presence* of sin (Rev 21:23, 27). But many Christians only seem to know about salvation in the past tense. They know that the cross has cleared their past account, that they have been forgiven and accepted by God because of what Jesus did on the cross. But they seem to think that they can now leave the cross behind and press on into the more positive blessings of the Christian life. 'No,' said Jesus. 'If you really want to be a true disciple you must take the cross along with you' (see Luke 14:27). Salvation is so much more than a free pardon for the past. It deals with those temptations that come from within, mentioned at the close of the last study.

What the cross signifies

Because it adorns a church building, or may be worn around the neck, we forget that the cross is no pretty emblem. Today we would talk of a hangman's noose or an electric chair, for the cross has to do with the execution of a criminal. Note three things that the cross signifies:

1. Shame

All that accompanied crucifixion, as well as the execution itself, was shameful as well as painful. The condemned man was scourged, mocked and spat upon (Mt 27:26–31). There was the procession to the place of execution through the hooting, jeering crowd, the prisoner carrying his cross (Jn 19:17). Finally he was stripped and nailed naked to the stake for all to see (Ps 22:17b). The wonder is not that the Son of God 'became obedient to death'—but that it was 'even death on a cross!' (Phil 2:8). Was there ever a death more shameful? Embracing the cross means coming to terms with 'the offence of the cross' (Gal 5:11).

2. Weakness

Again Psalm 22 puts these words prophetically into the lips of Christ:

> I am poured out like water, and all my bones are out of joint. My heart has turned to wax; it has melted away within me. My strength is dried up like a potsherd, and my tongue sticks to the roof of my mouth' (vv. 14–15).

The cross puts a man into a place of appalling weakness and helplessness. Paul, speaking of the risen Christ to the Corinthians, says, 'He is not weak in dealing with you, but is powerful among you. For to be sure, *he was*

crucified in weakness, yet he lives by God's power'
(2 Cor 13:3–4, italics mine). The cross is designed to
bring us to an end of our own resources and to a place of
total dependence on God.

3. Death

When Jesus spoke of bearing the cross, he wasn't talking
about playing a game of 'let's pretend'. His hearers
would know exactly what he meant. A man with ashen
face, struggling down the street with the cross on his
shoulder, goaded and kicked by a squad of Roman
soldiers, was a *man sentenced to death*. He was on his
way to execution. In that last scripture Paul said, 'We
felt the sentence of death.' Clearly they had the cross on
their shoulders. That this ugly emblem lies at the heart of
the Christian message should remind you that the gospel
was never intended to give you a mere spring-clean,
brighten you up, or make you a little more acceptable to
your Creator. It was designed to *finish you off*—so that
there could be 'a new creation' (2 Cor 5:17). The cross is
not to titivate, but to terminate. It offers a radical final
solution to the problem of on-going sin, and so opens the
way to bring us into all the blessings that lie on the
resurrection side of the cross.

Looking beyond

When we hear about being crucified with Christ, it all
sounds dark and forbidding. Who wants to tread such a
path? Christ is here our inspiration. 'Let us fix our eyes
on Jesus...who *for the joy set before him* endured the
cross, scorning its shame, and sat down at the right hand
of the throne of God' (Heb 12:2, italics mine). But
however could the prospect of the cross inspire any joy?
Because Jesus was *looking beyond the cross*, and seeing

what it was to accomplish. It was this that filled him with joy and took him triumphantly through the suffering and the shame. It will do exactly the same for us. Notice four tremendous things that the cross accomplishes for us.

1. It breaks the dominion of sin

To be falling into sin continually, having to confess it to God, and then draw on the grace of his forgiveness, is not the picture of the normal Christian life we find in the New Testament. It is sub-standard and we must not settle for it. 'Shall we go on sinning so that grace may increase? By no means!' says Paul. What then is the answer? Read on: 'We died to sin; how can we live in it any longer?' (Rom 6:1–2). The cross means death, and death is the only solution to the problem of recurring sin.

Note that Paul does *not* say: '*If* we die to sin we would not live in it.' He tells us straight—we *did* die to sin, so that continuing in it is not an option. Perhaps you respond, 'But I don't feel as though that old sinful self is dead, or if it's dead it won't lie down!' But God has not invited us to consult our feelings on the matter. He has not even suggested that we consider our track record or our past experience. He is telling us what happened when we were united by faith to Christ crucified: 'We died to sin.' In verse 6 of this same passage he says, 'We *know* that our old self was crucified with him.' How do we know? Only by the Holy Spirit revealing it to us.

A young woman, having asked Christ to be her Saviour, was told that she was now forgiven and accepted by God. But she said, 'I don't feel forgiven. How can I know it's true?' She was told, 'You will only know as you believe God's word. The Bible says, "Call on him and you will be saved. Confess your sins and you will be forgiven."' As she believed what God had said, she came into the good of what God had promised. It is just the same with dying to sin. We must believe what God says and not our own feelings.

2. *It brings power out of weakness*

We have already seen that the cross spells appalling weakness, but Jesus showed that it was the pathway to power. Only as he submitted to the way of the cross could he experience the power of the resurrection. It is that same resurrection power that we need to overcome the world. It is only ours as we tread the path he trod. So when Paul tells us about Jesus, that 'he was crucified in weakness, yet he lives by God's power', he then adds, 'Likewise, we are weak in him, yet by God's power we will live with him to serve you' (2 Cor 13:4).

The way to know this power is to take a positive attitude to everything that God permits in our lives to make us weak. We may not know for certain what was 'the thorn in the flesh' that Paul had to endure. We do know, however, why God did not remove it in answer to prayer. It was sent to keep him humble and to keep him weak (2 Cor 12:7–9). But the thorn was just one of the many things God used to strip Paul of his self-sufficiency and throw him back upon God (v.10). Things that we would have avoided were Paul's glad boast. To him they were the pathway to power and effectiveness.

Therefore, thank him for thy helplessness, beloved,
And if thou needst must long,
Let it be for the rest of utter weakness
In the arms for ever strong.
Long only that he make thee bare and empty,
Take all that is thine own,
Thy prowess and thy strength and thine endeavour,
And leave thee God alone.

3. It makes us fruitful

And which of us does not want to be fruitful? During the last week of his earthly life some Greeks requested an interview with Jesus. It seems he did not grant this request. Did he sense that they would present him with some attractive proposition to turn him from the path of the cross? 'The hour has come,' he said, 'for the Son of Man to be glorified'—but not the way that these men were in all probability proposing. He knew that the path to glory was via the cross, so he continued: 'I tell you the truth, unless an ear of wheat falls to the ground and dies, it remains only a single seed. But *if it dies,* it produces many seeds' (Jn 12:22–25, italics mine). What was Jesus saying?

Firstly, he was pointing to himself. He was the ear of wheat that had to fall into the ground and die. Centuries before it had been prophesied of him: 'Though the Lord makes his life a guilt offering, he will see his offspring' (Is 53:10). Here it was being fulfilled. It was looking beyond the cross and seeing the great harvest that would spring from his death. If Jesus had been unwilling to 'fall into the ground and die', he would have remained a single seed. By consenting to the cross, he would produce the harvest—'a great multitude that no-one could count' (Rev 7:9).

Jesus was also pointing out the path of fruitfulness for us. We too must be willing to be seen to fall into the ground and die if we are to bear much fruit. Strictly speaking, it is not the seed but the outer husk that dies in the process of germination. So Paul says, 'We always carry around *in our body* the death of Jesus, so that the life of Jesus may also be revealed in our body' (2 Cor 4:10, italics mine). It is by the Spirit that we must learn to 'put to death the misdeeds of the body' (Rom 8:13). As 'death is at work in us... life is at work' in others (2 Cor 4:12).

4. It is the pathway to glory

This is not something we may only experience when we get to heaven. We may know it in measure now if we have embraced the cross. Says Peter, 'If you are insulted because of the name of Christ... the Spirit of glory and of God rests on you' (1 Pet 4:14). Christians who have suffered much for Christ's sake usually have a joy, a radiance and a beauty in their faces that is not of this world. They seem to carry with them a sense of God. This is only a foretaste of the glory which we are to enjoy when we enter God's presence.

Probably the greatest temptation Jesus had to face in his earthly life was to take a path to glory that bypassed the cross. In the wilderness temptation the devil offered him all the kingdoms of the world and their glory if he would worship him (Lk 4:5-7). Jesus knew that one day they would all be his, but first he must 'face death for everyone'. It was because of his obedience to death that God has exalted him to the highest place (Phil 2:9). There was no short cut for him (Lk 24:26), and there is none for us (2 Tim 2:11-12a). The cross is still the only path to glory.

Conclusion

So if you would know—

> Abiding victory over sin
> God's power made perfect in weakness
> A life of abundant fruitfulness
> And the hope of glory

—you must come to terms with the cross as a present experience. If you have already been baptized in water this will not require you doing something that has not been done, but recognizing something that Christ has already done for you.

Memorize

For we know that our old self was crucified with him so that the body of sin might be rendered powerless, that we should no longer be slaves to sin (Rom 6:6).

Home task

1. 'Sin shall not be your master' (Rom 6:14). That is both a command and a promise. If there are temptations that regularly floor you, you have not yet fully embraced the cross. Read again your memory verse. It says, 'We *know*....' That is more than a mental knowing, it comes by the revelation of the Holy Spirit. Call on God to give you that revelation. You will know that you have it when you can say boldly and with conviction, 'I *know* that my old self was crucified with Christ.' Don't move on to the next point until you can do this.

2. Read Romans 6:12–14. Says Paul, 'Do not offer the parts of your body to sin...' (v.13). Instead do two things:

a) 'Offer yourselves to God.' But how? 'As those who have been brought from death to life.' Do that right now. Surrender yourself totally to God, in the faith that the old self is dead, and that you are a new person in Christ (see Romans 12:1).

b) 'Offer the parts of your body to him.' Think of what part of your body is involved in each area of temptation. 'Here is my mind, Lord, that used to think wrong thoughts. I present it to you as an instrument of right-eousness.' Go through them all one by one, and remember, you are not under law—you keeping it up—but under grace—God keeping you up (v.14).

For further study

1. This will help you to discover the secret of spiritual power through the cross. Read again 2 Corinthians 12:7–10. Note Paul's list of the hard things he had to face (v.10). They were not sins, but weaknesses and testing situations. Compile your own list of the things that you find hard, like shyness and self-consciousness, difficulty in expressing yourself, being ridiculed at work, opposition at home, and all the things that make it hard to follow Jesus. Under the list write what God says about them all (v.9). Ask God to help you believe what he says. The proof will be when you can:

(a) Boast about your weaknesses instead of moaning about them (v.9).

(b) Delight in them instead of shrinking from them (v.10).

(c) Know that Christ's power has been made perfect in your weakness (v.9).

2. The cross is the path to glory. See how this is illustrated in the life of Joseph (Gen 37, 39—40). Make a note of the events in these chapters that you think would have worked the cross into Joseph's life. What particular weaknesses do you think God was dealing with in Joseph in order to fit him for the throne (Gen 37:2, 5–11)?

Understanding God's Ways

Read
Hebrews 12:4–11.

Something very important

Though God redeemed Israel out of Egypt and made them his people, they did not understand his ways. They saw him do great things for them in deliverance and miraculous provision. They also saw him act towards them in judgement and discipline. Moses understood what lay behind these deeds—God's *ways*—but the people didn't: 'He made known his *ways* to Moses, his *deeds* to the people of Israel' (Ps 103:7, italics mine). That speaks of two very different levels of understanding. Knowing the ways of God is how we come to know God. See how Moses reached out for that deeper understanding in Exodus 33:13.

At the end of the wilderness wanderings, Moses said to the people: 'Remember how the Lord your God led you all the way in the desert....He humbled you, causing you to hunger and then feeding you with manna' (Deut 8:2–3). Causing them to hunger and feeding them with manna were both acts of God, but it was much easier to understand God's 'deeds' in feeding them than to understand why he suffered them to hunger. In this study we are going to focus on the ways of God that we find difficult, the disciplining of our lives. This is something vital if we are to mature.

God is sovereign

This means that God not only governs the affairs of men, but that he possesses absolute authority. He acts, he intervenes, he permits, he promotes, he forbids and he overrules—in order to accomplish his purpose. He doesn't do all this—circumstances permitting, or human beings permitting, or Satan permitting. He does it all regardless (Is 14:27). That's what we mean by absolute authority. He may use men, even wicked men (Acts 2:23). He may even use Satan (see under 'But don't see him too big', Study 10). The fact is, 'He does as he pleases with the powers of heaven and the peoples of the earth. No-one can hold back his hand or say to him: "What have you done?"' (Dan 4:35).

The New Testament bears equal witness to this truth of the sovereignty of God. We are introduced to one 'who works out everything in conformity with the purpose of his will' (Eph 1:11). And the circumstances of a believer's life are so perfectly controlled by God that 'in all things God works for the good for those who love him' (Rom 8:28). We have no problem in believing this when God's ways obviously work out for our happiness and prosperity. But what do we feel when they bring disappointment and adversity? This is where we must learn to sing the song of Moses and the song of the Lamb: not only, 'Great and marvellous are your deeds, Lord God Almighty,' but also, *'Just and true are your ways*, King of the Ages' (Rev 15:3, italics mine). To have full faith in God's sovereignty is essential for a proper understanding of God's ways.

God, Satan or chance?

How do you react when unforseen events overtake you?
If it was a legacy for £10,000 left you by Aunt Fanny, you
would no doubt bless God and bless Aunt Fanny. But if,
as in the case of a friend of mine, you learn that you have
lost £10,000 as a result of a business failure you may find
there are conflicting reactions. Do you simply dismiss it
as 'bad luck', one of those misfortunes that could happen
to anyone?

The fact is you are not 'anyone', but someone very
special to God, one of his children for whom he takes a
fatherly responsibility. If we have grasped the truth of
God's sovereignty we will know that our affairs are not
subject to luck, fate or chance, whether good or bad
(Rom 8:28).

Of course you might feel it was your own silly fault for
agreeing hastily to invest in that firm, or in not seeking
the advice of others. But the fact is, you were still in the
hands of One who is willing and able to intervene and
over-rule your foolish decisions—and often does. Why
did he not do it this time?

Was it Satan? If you grasped the lesson of Job's misfortunes (Study 10) you will know that though Satan
possesses supernatural power and is our sworn enemy,
he is only permitted to operate within certain clearly-
defined boundaries. These are laid down by God, and
God has purposes of blessing in all that he permits. In
Job 1:6–12 and 2:1–6 we are told about the argument
between God and Satan as to whether Job was the good
man that God said he was. After that Satan is never
mentioned again in the book. Job came right through
into victory, and his health and fortunes were restored,

and so far as we know he never knew that Satan had any part in the attacks on his possessions, his family and his health. When God shows us that we are under satanic attack, then we resist him by faith. At other times we deal with God, as Job did, and whether or not Satan is involved need not concern us.

Does God punish us?

The answer to this is 'Yes' and 'No'. If we are thinking of punishment as divine condemnation for sins committed, the answer is 'No'. The ungodly will suffer this on the day of judgement (Mt 25:41, 46), but the true believer 'has eternal life and will not be condemned; he has crossed over from death to life' (Jn 5:24; cf Rom 8:1).

But if we mean, 'Does God punish us by corrective discipline?' the answer is 'Yes'. Scripture teaches us that just as surely as a human father who truly loves his son will not spare the rod (Prov 13:24), so our heavenly Father uses his rod with his children (Deut 8:5). You will have seen from the reading that this is a New Testament as much as an Old Testament concept.

A man noticed that some of his choice desert apples were disappearing from his orchard at the bottom of the garden. That evening he saw a figure among the trees, and when the young culprit was apprehended, it was his own boy. Had the thief been a stranger, he would have rung the police, but since it was his son, he said, 'Go to your bedroom and wait for me there.' In due course 'the board of education' came into painful contact with the 'seat of learning'.

When we sin we are not handed over to the law to face the Judge of all the earth. Christ's death on the cross has fully satisfied the demands of the law on our behalf. But that doesn't mean we can sin with impunity because we are believers. There is still the discipline and correction of our heavenly Father (1 Cor 11:32).

The discipline of the Lord

There are some things in our reading that we must understand if we are to respond aright to God's dealings with us.

1. Expression of love

Look at Hebrews 12:8: 'If you are not disciplined (and everyone undergoes discipline), then you are illegitimate children and not true sons.' From the beginning of Scripture through to the end that's the way discipline is viewed (Rev 3:19). If we ever speak of God 'punishing' his children we must understand that his action is a proof of his loving commitment to bring us through into maturity. This verse 8 is teaching us that it is *the absence* of God's fatherly discipline and correction in our lives that should give us cause for concern. We should have to ask ourselves, 'Am I a true son?' God doesn't discipline the unsaved and the ungodly, any more than the man with the orchard would have felt free to apply the stick to someone else's son. Discipline is the mark of God's special concern.

2. No exceptions

Did you notice those three words in verse 8, 'Everyone undergoes discipline'? Certainly not every one of the Father's children are worldly, wayward or backslidden, but all are disciplined. So not all discipline is because of unrighteous acts. Job's friends made the mistake of thinking this about Job, though God had expressed the very opposite when he spoke to Satan. But there was still a purifying of his character which God had to accomp-

117

lish. Even when we are generally living in victory and
walking in the Spirit, thoughts, motives and attitudes
need to be purified (2 Cor 10:5).

3. It hurts!

The closing verse of our reading says: 'No discipline
seems pleasant at the time, but painful.' Our older
versions generally use the old-fashioned word 'chastise-
ment' instead of discipline. This is the word that
describes the fatherly 'laying on of hands' in the case of
the son caught stealing his father's apples. It is not meant
to be pleasant, it's meant to hurt. Sometimes the pain is
mental, sometimes physical. With Job it was both. But
far more painful than the physical afflictions of being
covered with sores was the mental pain of being wrongfully accused by 'the friends' who had apparently come
to comfort him. One thing is certain. Whatever affliction
God orders or permits, it is always an expression of his
unfailing love, and always for our ultimate blessing
(Lam 3:33).

4. For our profit

That is what verse 11 in our reading goes on to say:
'Later on, however, it produces a harvest of righteousness and peace for those who have been trained by it.'
Not just a little fruit, but a *harvest*. Take Job. God had
blessed the early part of Job's life. According to Satan
that was the only reason why Job served God (1:9–11).
Satan, the accuser, implied that it was cupboard love. But
'The Lord blessed the latter part of Job's life more than
the first' (Job 42:12). That doesn't only mean that God
increased his possessions. He had had a conviction, even
in the midst of his trial, that God was refining him, and
that he would come forth as gold (Job 23:10), and that's

exactly what happened. God changed a man who was
outwardly righteous into one who was inwardly holy.
'God disciplines us for our good, that we may share in his
holiness' (Heb 12:10).

Handling it aright

'You intended to harm me, but God intended it for
good' (Gen 50:20). That's what Joseph said years after
to his brothers who had sold him into slavery. Whether
our misfortunes come to us through the malice of the
devil or the evil intentions of men, it is always true—
'God intended it for good.' That is another way of
expressing Romans 8:28. But whether God's intention is
fulfilled depends on our reacting aright. Would Joseph
have ever qualified for the throne—would he have ever
become the instrument of blessing and salvation that
God intended, if he had allowed his brothers' cruel
injustice to fill him with bitterness and resentment? In
verses 5 and 6 of our reading we have two negative
commands which teach us how to respond aright to the
Lord's discipline:

1. Do not make light of it

This is how we may be tempted to react. We shrug it off.
We explain it away. 'Surely this couldn't be God saying
anything to me.' It is humbling to acknowledge that God
is disciplining us and adjusting us, so we dismiss the
thought and look for natural explanations. This verse is
saying, 'Take God's discipline seriously. Things don't
happen in your life accidentally.' The right response, as
our reading reminds us, is one of submission (v.9). See
how positively and believingly the psalmist responded to
his trials (Ps 119:71, 75).

2. *Do not lose heart*

This is the other, opposite temptation. We don't shrug it off or deny that it is God, but we take it badly. We feel that God is being harsh and unloving. 'Doesn't he understand all that I've been through already?' We let feelings of resentment lodge in our hearts. If our trial has come through God's people, we may have resentment towards them, but it's really against God that we have these feelings. This is what happened to Job. His 'friends' with their false accusations stirred him up, and then out came his words about God being unjust (Job 9:15–18). In the midst of his fiery affliction poor Job lost heart altogether. He wished he had never been born, and only wanted to die (Job 3:11, 20–21).

Job felt the way he did because he couldn't see the purpose of grace that God had in mind for him. He could only hear the devil's whisper, 'You are going through this because God hates you and has abandoned you.' Have you ever heard Satan whisper that? God says, 'No, you are going through this because I love you and accept you as my son [see Hebrews 12:6–7]. And because you are my son, I want you to bear the family likeness, that is, share my holiness [see verse 10]. What you have had before has been firstfruits, but I want to give you a harvest' [see verse 11].

Memorize

> *No discipline seems pleasant at the time, but painful. Later on, however, it produces a harvest of righteousness and peace for those who have been trained by it* (Heb 12:11).

Home task

1. Note some of the ways in which God changes us through trials and testings. What are the changes described by the following scriptures? Jot them down. Are you able to identify with some of them from your own experience?

(a) Psalm 107:17-20.

(b) 1 Peter 1:6-7.

(c) 1 Peter 5:10.

(d) Hebrews 12:10.

(e) 2 Corinthians 1:3-4.

(f) 2 Corinthians 4:17.

2. Are you going through some discipline of the Lord right now?

(a) Make sure that you are not falling into either of the two traps mentioned in Hebrews 12:5-6.

(b) Do you understand what God is wanting to do in you through this testing? If not, ask him to show you, and then call on him for grace to respond aright to his working in you.

For further study

In 1 Corinthians 11:17-34 Paul speaks of the way the Corinthians had been misbehaving when they celebrated the Lord's Supper in church.

(a) Write down the things for which Paul reprimanded them (vv.20-22).

(b) How is their behaviour described in verse 27, and then in verse 29?

(c) This had serious physical consequences for the believers concerned. What were they (v.30)? The last phrase in this verse becomes clear by its use in 15:6 of this same epistle.

(d) These consequences are described as being 'disciplined' by the Lord (v.32). How else are they described in this verse and in the previous verse?

(e) What does all this teach us about how we should celebrate the Lord's Supper?

Enjoying Spiritual Nourishment

Read
Psalm 1.

The art of meditation

This is the theme of our study, but it has nothing to do with TM (transcendental meditation). TM claims to be a scientific method of exploring into the deepest levels of your own being, and so finding freedom from stress and peace of mind. But it is a deception. Though it claims to be non-religious, the mantras that are recited are prayers to Hindu gods and the practice involves opening up one's self to spirits other than the Holy Spirit. The meditation advocated in the Bible does not focus on ourselves, but on God and his word. Most of the teaching on this theme is in the Old Testament, but it is equally a New Testament practice. Our handling of scriptures may involve hearing, reading, memorizing, studying and even singing, but meditation is the major means of our spiritual nourishment.

An Old Testament picture

As soon as God had delivered Israel from Egypt he spoke to them about their daily food, 'bread from heaven', that he promised to supply. They were to gather it each day, and this was to be a discipline, a test of obedience (Ex 16:4). Gathering the manna was not simply something for leaders or a special squad to do. Each redeemed Israelite had to gather it. Nor was it an annual, monthly, or even weekly event. It was to be gathered *daily*, for it could not be kept (vv.19–20). This 'bread from heaven' is a picture of Christ (Jn 6:32–35). It is equally a picture of God's word, for feeding on God's word is feeding on Christ. So no one who has been redeemed is too young in the faith to start gathering his daily manna. If this was an important discipline for the Israelites (Deut 8:3–5), it is equally so for us.

A farming picture

1. Chewing the cud

We have all watched cows grazing. Most of the time they are not nibbling, but lying down endlessly munching. This is called 'chewing the cud' or ruminating. They chew the grass over and over to get all the nourishment out of it. The Oxford dictionary tells us that to ruminate also means 'to revolve, to turn over and over in the mind, to meditate deeply upon, to consider with a view to subsequent action'. Biblical meditation, however, is more than a mental exercise. It includes the human spirit, and requires the aid of the Holy Spirit.

2. Mind or spirit

Bible study and Bible meditation often overlap, but there is distinction. Study puts the emphasis on the mind. It is an intellectual activity, also needing the aid of the Holy Spirit. But not all believers have the mental equipment to cope with Bible study. In meditation, though the mind is used, the focus is more on the human spirit, and *all believers* must learn this art. Intellectual ability, yielded to God, is valuable, but we don't need it to hear God speak to us through his word. When that happens the simple become wise in the estimate of heaven (Ps 19:7).

3. The secret of its effectiveness

Sitting on the conference platform was a big man wearing a rough suit, his head on one side and his mouth half open. 'Who is that?' asked a young man in the congregation, turning to his friend.

'He's the speaker,' came the surprising answer. 'He's a farm labourer who left school at the age of twelve.'

The young man groaned, and then settled down to endure what was to come!

The speaker commenced by quoting a verse of that old hymn 'O Christ what burdens bowed thy head'. Suddenly the place was filled with the presence of God. Then he opened his Bible and gave the assembled company 'honey out of the rock'. So impressed was the young man that he asked the preacher afterwards where he got such great truths. He told him that he rose early in the morning, lit a candle, got dressed, and then read one or two verses over and over again. Then he put his coat on and walked the country lanes, trusting the Holy Spirit to put the truth that was in his head into his heart. 'That's where I get it all' he concluded. Oh yes, he had been educated all right—in the school of meditation— personally tutored by the Holy Spirit.

The process of meditation

This consists of three phases which God uses to impart truth:

1. Apprehension

This initial phase involves spiritual understanding or insight (Ps 119:99). Remember in the parable of the sower, Jesus spoke first of how the seed fell on the path. He said that this spoke of those who heard the message and did not *understand* it (Mt 13:4, 19). He was speaking of spiritual understanding that comes by the revelation of the Holy Spirit. Notice the contrast with what Paul says about us believers who *have* the Spirit (1 Cor 2:12), with what he says a moment later about the unbeliever who *has not* the Spirit (v.14).

2. Assimilation

This is more than spiritual understanding. To feed the spirit it is not enough to take in spiritual food, it must be digested. This is the heart of the meditation process. You can eat a lot, so the medics tell us, and still be undernourished if the body fails to assimilate food. If we are reading the Bible regularly, receiving much teaching, but not growing or maturing, it is because our spiritual digestive system is undeveloped or out of order. 'You are what you eat' is the provocative title of a book on health foods. It is a reminder that your food becomes you in terms of bone, blood cells, tissue, etc. Equally our spiritual food forms our spiritual character when we assimilate it. Good spiritual digestion gives soul satisfaction (Ps 63:5–6). Paul is talking about this in Colossians 3:16.

3. Application

Finally there is a practical outworking of the process of meditation. As well as building up our characters and nourishing our faith, there is an adjustment of our lives. On the positive side, we assimilate the word that we may conform our lives to it. We meditate on it with a view to obeying it (Josh 1:8). To put it differently, we become doers as well as feeders (Jas 1:23–25).

On the negative side we let the word of God convict and purge us where we have failed to obey it. David records how he kept quiet about something that he should have confessed to God, but as he meditated the fire of conviction burned (Ps 39:2–3). He later confessed to God (vv.7–11).

Some of the benefits

There are five that came in our reading of Psalm 1. These should be sufficient to motivate us.

1. Enjoyment

'His delight is in the law of the Lord' (v.2). Though there is a discipline involved in getting down to meditation, when you do it, there are delightful surprises in store. To the psalmist, discovering God's promises was like tasting honey or finding treasure (Ps 119:103, 162). This same psalmist has no fear that he will neglect God's word, because it is his delight (v.16). No wonder he bursts out, 'Oh, how I love your law! I meditate on it all day long' (v.97).

2. Nourishment

'He is like a tree planted by streams of water' (v.3), so that the roots are well nourished. A sickly Christian is almost always undernourished. He has not learned, or has neglected to feed his soul on, God's word. This was one of the first lessons the Old Testament prophets had to learn. Ezekiel was told to eat the scroll which had words from God on it before he could go and speak to the house of Israel (Ezek 3:1–4). Similarly Jeremiah records: 'When your words came ['were found' in AV and RSV], I ate them' (Jer 15:16). God's words 'being found' suggests that Jeremiah had made a discovery, one that comes by the revelation of the Spirit. Only when the truth reaches the heart is it assimilated and we are nourished.

3. Fruit bearing

'A tree...which yields its fruit in season' (v.3). We saw that feeding on the manna was a picture both of feeding on Christ and feeding on his word. The parable of the vine emphasizes abiding or remaining in Christ, and Christ remaining in you. The result? Fruit! But Jesus linked this with his word when he said, 'If you remain in me, and *my words* remain in you' (Jn 15:7, italics mine)—you will be very fruitful, for you will always get your prayers answered. Christ is the source of our life (Jn 14:19) and the word is also the source of our life (Jn 6:63). If we try hard to remain in Christ while neglecting to dwell in his word, we will court failure and frustration. If we meditate in his word we shall be truly fruitful.

4. Healing

'Whose leaf does not whither' (v.3). What has that to do with healing? In Ezekiel's vision of the river flowing from the sanctuary he saw fruit trees on the banks, and was told, 'Their fruit will serve for food and their leaves for healing' (Ezek 47:12; also Rev 22:2).

Jesus said, 'These signs will accompany those who believe...they will place their hands on sick people, and they will get well' (Mt 16:17–18). Note, this was not said of leaders or those with special gifts. It is a promise to all believing believers. Sharing in a ministry of healing whether spiritual, emotional, mental or physical is open to us all.

5. Success

Finally, 'Whatever he does prospers' (v.3). What does that mean? 'The Lord was with Joseph and he prospered...the Lord gave him success in everything he did'—even though he was a slave (Gen 39:2–3).

To prosper in the estimate of heaven is to have God with you so that everything you do is successful. What Christian does not want that?

Notice how God promised exactly this to Joshua, that God would be with him, and that he would prosper, but with exactly the same condition as the man in Psalm 1 who meditated on God's word day and night, and obeyed it implicitly (Josh 1:5, 8).

Getting down to the job

1. Reading and meditating

If you cannot give time to meditate separately from your daily reading, you can quite successfully combine the two. It is a good way to start. First, ask God where in the Scripture he wants you to read and meditate. Try to avoid flitting from one passage to another. Instead, meditate consecutively. Read your passage slowly, looking to God to speak. Soon a phrase or thought will arrest you. Stop your reading and start to meditate. Turn it over and over in your mind. It may take you to other verses or incidents in the Bible.

2. Uttering and muttering

The two main words in Hebrew for 'meditate' also mean 'to speak, commune, or even to mutter or talk to yourself'. This is not the first sign of madness! David often did it (Ps 42:5). God said to Joshua, 'Do not let this

Book of the Law depart from your mouth [that is, don't
stop uttering it]; meditate on it day and night' (Josh 1:8).

Mouthing and meditating go together (Ps 19:14).
Uttering and muttering are not simply to fix truth in your
mind. They are part of the digestive process; you are
assimilating the truth. Often it develops into confession,
prayer or praise.

3. Record your findings

Even when it reaches your heart, there is no guarantee
that your mind will retain it, so use a notebook to record
the fruit of your meditation. Writing will also help to
clarify your thinking and it will order your thoughts so
that you can better share these good things with others.

Memorize

> *Do not let this Book of the Law depart from your
> mouth; meditate on it day and night, so that you may
> be careful to do everything written in it. Then you will
> be prosperous and successful* (Josh 1:8).

Home task

Choose a portion of Scripture for meditation. Ask God
to guide you to the right passage. If nothing springs
readily to mind, turn to your last Scripture reading and
follow the instructions I have given under 'Getting down
to the job'. When you have fixed on a verse or sentence,
read it over and over again, but don't bite off more than
you can chew. One verse should give you plenty of
scope.

Pray continually, 'Lord speak to me the truths I need
to hear. Feed me with the food you see I need.' As

thoughts come, write them down in your notebook—and don't forget to utter or mutter! You will need to allow twenty to thirty minutes for this. Your meditations may well lead to confessions of failure, to thanksgiving, or to supplication for yourself and others. It may help you to record the gist of these too in your notebook.

For further study

1. What are the main things that God has taught you in this study on meditation? When you have noted them down, write underneath what action you have determined to take to carry out this teaching.

2. Psalm 119, as we have already noted, has much to teach us on meditation. If you are using the NIV you will find 'meditate' occurs eight times. Note down each verse and what it teaches:

(a) The situations and circumstances in which the Psalmist meditates.

(b) His testimony as to what meditation does for him.

(c) The conditions that make for successful meditating.

Maintaining the Fullness

Read
Acts 6:1–8.

Introduction

This study is written for those who know that they have
received the Baptism in the Holy Spirit. If you have not
yet come into that experience I would commend to you
Study 6 in the earlier course, *Living God's Way*. If
necessary, seek help from a mature Christian you trust
who has been baptized in the Spirit, who will counsel and
help you. You are not yet ready for this study, because
you cannot learn to maintain a fullness that you have
never received.

Fullness must be maintained

Experiencing 'baptism in the Spirit' doesn't immediately
lock us into a place of spirituality and effectiveness from
which we can never lapse. On the contrary, because we
have been endued with power, we have become a greater
threat to the enemy, and he will redouble his efforts to
bring us down. Notice what happened to our Lord after

the Holy Spirit came upon him at the Jordan (Mt 3:16—4:3).

It is sad but true that believers *can*, and in some cases *do*, lose the blessing of the anointing of the Holy Spirit. David had a real fear of this after his grievous sin over Bathsheba, as we see from what he says in his prayer of repentance (Ps 51:11). He would have remembered what happened to Samson, one of Israel's judges, on whom the Spirit came in power (Judg 14:6; 16:20–21). Or even more vividly, what happened to his predecessor, King Saul. David always acknowledged him as 'the Lord's anointed', for he had had a powerful enduement of the Spirit (1 Sam 10:9–10; 16:14).

Charisma or character?

Charisma (meaning 'gift of grace') emphasizes what we *do*. *Character* emphasizes what we *are*. When you look at what the Bible teaches about the baptism of the Holy Spirit, that it is an enduement of power (Lk 24:49; Acts 1:8), and that it brings spiritual gifts, the emphasis is clearly upon charisma and what we do. Notice that it was normally received by new converts. They were not required to reach a special standard of holiness, become mature or knowledgeable before they received the Holy Spirit (Acts 2:38–39; 8:14–17). Jesus had promised that his heavenly Father would give the Holy Spirit to those who asked him (Lk 11:13), provided, as always that they asked in faith (Gal 3:14). It was as simple as that. However, though the Galatians and the Corinthians had received the Spirit by faith, the Galatians lapsed into legalism, and the Corinthians into carnality (worldliness).

What we must understand clearly is that how the blessing is *obtained* is one thing, how it is *maintained* is something else. As we go on living the Christian life we receive more light (understanding of truth). God then requires us to walk (conduct our daily lives) in that greater light that we have received (1 Jn 1:6–7). The crisis of receiving must be followed by the process of maintaining and increasing. The renewal of the Spirit is not a once-for-all experience. It must be renewed day by day (2 Cor 4:16). There is no doubt that the Ephesian church had had the crisis. They had been marked with the Spirit's seal (Eph 1:13). We are actually told how the twelve foundation members of that church had had this experience through the laying on of Paul's hands, and immediately following their water baptism (Acts 19: 4–7). So when he exhorts them to be 'filled with the Spirit' (Eph 5:18), he is not emphasizing the crisis but the process. It could be translated 'be being filled' or 'go on being filled with the Spirit'. In other words, let your experience of 'being filled' become a state of 'being full'.

Understanding 'Spirit-filled'

When Scripture uses 'filled' in connection with the Holy Spirit, it is emphasizing quality rather than quantity. When we say, 'That man is Spirit-filled,' we are not describing *measure*—how much he has of the Spirit—so much as *influence*—how much the Spirit has of him.

When Jesus spoke in the Nazareth synagogue, the hearers were 'filled with fury' (Lk 6:11, RSV). That is to say, they lost all self-control, anger took over and they behaved like men 'possessed'. Anger characterized their words and actions.

To be Spirit-filled is to be Spirit-possessed. Your speech and behaviour take on the characteristics of the Holy Spirit, who is both holy and spiritual. Let us ask ourselves some questions about someone who has received the Holy Spirit and even come into an experience of spiritual gifts.

1. If he is not walking with God any more, is he Spirit-filled?

2. Though he may attend church, participate in meetings, etc, if he is not a witness for Christ, and his life lacks power and effectiveness (Acts 1:8) is he Spirit-filled?

3. If he engages in many forms of Christian service but there is little or no lasting fruit, is he Spirit-filled?

4. If his fellow believers find him as difficult to get on with as they did before he received 'the baptism' is he Spirit-filled?

5. If he has the gifts of the Spirit, but little of the fruit of the Spirit, is he Spirit-filled?

The Corinthian church had received the power of the Holy Spirit and were moving strongly in spiritual gifts. Paul thanked God for this (1 Cor 1:4–7), and encouraged them to press on into greater gifts (1 Cor 12:31; 14:1, 12), but he says reprovingly, 'I could not address you as spiritual but as worldly—mere infants...acting like mere men' (1 Cor 3:1, 3). Hardly the description of a Spirit-filled company! They had not maintained what they had obtained. The crisis had not been followed by the process. They had received the Spirit but were not walking in the Spirit. They were strong in charisma, but weak in character.

Christ is our model

The marks of a Spirit-filled person are seen first in our Lord Jesus.

1. Spirit-led

At his baptism the Spirit came upon him. Then we read, 'Jesus, *full of the Holy Spirit*, returned from the Jordan and was *led by the Spirit* into the desert' (Lk 4:1, italics mine). So a Spirit-filled man is led by the Spirit. He does not initiate a lot of Christian activity, and then ask God to bless it. He lets God do the initiating and he does the responding. This marked the whole of Jesus' earthly ministry (Jn 5:19).

2. Spirit-empowered

After the wilderness temptation, this Spirit-filled man 'returned to Galilee in *the power of the Spirit*' (Lk 4:14, italics mine). There is no evidence in Scripture that he displayed this power before the Holy Spirit came on him. We know that all his life he was 'holy, blameless, pure, set apart from sinners' (Heb 7:26), but for those first thirty years, we do not read of one sermon being preached, one disciple being made, or one miracle being performed. After the Jordan experience, however, what a change! Wherever he went, the power of the Spirit accompanied his ministry and made it effective. So after Pentecost, Peter could even address a foreigner like the Roman Centurion, and say, 'You know what has happened throughout Judea...how God anointed Jesus of Nazareth with the Holy Spirit and power, and how he went around doing good and healing all who are under the power of the devil' (Acts 10:37–38). Had not Jesus told the disciples himself that the evidence that the Holy Spirit had come upon them would be *power* (Acts 1:8)? Power which would make their witness and their ministry effective.

A man was pushing his cycle to the top of a steep hill. A motorcycle zoomed past him to the top, and when he arrived there, puffing and panting, the motorcycle was parked and the owner, looking cool and relaxed, was enjoying the view. Said the push-cyclist, ruefully eyeing the Suzuki, 'The difference between your machine and mine is yours is "spirit-filled"!'

Power is an indispensible mark of being Spirit-filled. But as the fullness is maintained, we should expect the power to be increased, as it was with Saul of Tarsus (Acts 9:18, 20–22).

3. Grace and truth

Jesus was not only full of power, he was also 'full of grace and truth' (Jn 1:14). This was the 'character' aspect of his fullness, the perfect balance to the 'charisma' aspect. Power unrelated to godliness may produce results, but no lasting blessing. How unacceptable would have been the miracles of Jesus if they had been devoid of grace. How dubious would his healings have been if we never read, 'Jesus moved with compassion' healed the sick. He wept at Lazarus' tomb before he called him back to life. Grace and power are essential ingredients of the Spirit-filled life.

There was a man who turned up in a Christian circle I know and dazzled everyone with his charisma. When he laid hands on people for the Holy Spirit, they were filled and spoke in tongues. When he prayed for the sick, they were healed. He had remarkable words of knowledge about people's situations. Soon everyone was deferring to him as the leader. But he was a phoney. He was a married man, and when his colleagues heard about the women in his life, his lying and dishonesty over money, they could not believe it. Charisma is dangerous without character.

Balaam was a prophet. He had a reputation for predicting things that came to pass (Num 22:6). He certainly heard God and spoke words from God. He was so at home in the supernatural that when the Lord opened the donkey's mouth to speak to him, he answered him back without batting an eyelid (Num

22:29)! But his character was crooked, and in the end he was slain by the Israelites and branded as an occultist (Josh 13:22).

Christ shows the way

Even as Jesus demonstrates the perfect Spirit-filled life, he also reveals the open secret of how it is to be maintained.

1. Righteousness and wickedness

'You have loved righteousness and hated wickedness; therefore God... has set you above your companions by anointing you with the oil of joy' (Heb 1:9). Back of this unique and remarkable fullness that Jesus enjoyed was a passion for what pleased God and a loathing for the things God hated. When his Father anointed him at the Jordan, God declard audibly, 'You are my Son, whom I love; with you I am well pleased' (Lk 3:22). And because all through his earthly course he never deviated from this, and never compromised his convictions, the Spirit continued to rest on him in power. But there was also the element of faith:

2. Drinking from the brook

Did you know that the Son of Man had to live by faith just as we are required to do? It is said of the coming Messiah, 'He will drink from a brook beside the way; therefore he will lift up his head' (Ps 110:7). Alongside the God-directed path that followed was the brook, 'the supply of the Spirit', needed for living as well as for serving. Had he strayed from the way, he would have been out of touch with the brook. Of course he never did, because of what we have already observed in (1). Whenever he grew weary, or was assaulted by the devil, or tempted to discouragement, or challenged by the need or opportunity, he simply drank from the brook, and pressed on with head held high. Jesus was living out what he had taught the woman by the well, that the Holy Spirit would be 'a spring of water welling up to eternal life' (Jn 4:14), continually renewing, refreshing and invigorating the inner man. Drinking is receiving the Spirit by faith, and it is not something you do once-for-all. 'There is no such thing as a once-for-all fullness. It is a moment-by-moment faith in a moment-by-moment Saviour, for a moment-by-moment cleansing and a moment-by-moment filling' (Dr Charles Inwood). That's how the fullness is maintained.

Memorize

> *If a man is thirsty, let him come to me and drink. Whoever believes* [present continuous tense] *in me, as the Scripture has said, streams of living water will flow from within him* (Jn 7:37–38).

Home task

1. If you believe you have been filled with the Spirit, check yourself out to know whether you are still full of the Holy Spirit, or have become a leaky vessel. Go over the three points under 'Christ is our model' and see how your own Christian life measures up to these three marks of being Spirit-filled. Where you sense that you come short, seek God for a renewing, or a fresh infilling, of the Spirit by means of repentance (for sin and failure) and faith to lay hold of God's grace which is abundantly available.

2. Note that the blessing of the Spirit is maintained

and increased by the same principles as it was initially received. Pick out from the following scriptures, the two main conditions for receiving:

(a) Acts 5:32, cf John 14:15–16

(b) Galatians 3:14, cf John 7:38

Consider carefully whether there has been failure on your part to continue to fulfil these two key principles. Talk to God freely and frankly over these areas of your life. Here is a simple resolution that you may like to use:

'I resolve by the grace of God and his enabling that I will continue day by day to _____ and to ____ _____ [the two key conditions] in every area of my Christian life.

For further study

1. Jesus promised his followers power. It has been said, 'Power is dangerous stuff in the hands of those not qualified to handle it.' Write down in your notebook:

(a) Whether you think this is a valid and important statement in relation to the power of the Holy Spirit, and if so why.

(b) What do you think the safeguards are? Try to support your statements from Scripture.

2. King Saul is one of the saddest cases in Scripture of a man who lost his spiritual anointing. The following scriptures tell the story of how his decline began: 1 Samuel 13:5–14; 14:24–28, 36–45; 15:1–35. Pick out the places where he went wrong, and note down any lessons or warnings that you believe God has for you in the story.

SECTION 3

Living in the World

In it—But not of it

Read

John 15:18–21; 17:13–19.

Introduction

We are taking a look at 'the world' in this study. It is important to understand what Scripture means by 'the world', as the term is used in different ways. Also what it means to be 'in it, but not of it'.

Defining 'the world'

Scripture speaks of the world in at least three distinct ways:

1. The world of nature

This demonstrates God's wisdom and power. It should always move us, as it did the psalmist, to recognize God's greatness and our nothingness (Ps 8:3–4), and so to worship him as the great Creator (Ps 104). Here we have to watch that we do not worship the creation rather than the Creator. From antiquity this has been the curse of heathenism (Job 31:26–28). God warned Israel against idolatry (Deut 4:15–19).

2. *The world of men*

This is 'the world' that 'God so loved' and for which 'he gave his one and only Son' (Jn 3:16). This is the world that we must learn to love too, even in all its sinfulness, if we are to play any part in winning it (2 Cor 5:14, 20). It comes down to loving individual men and women who are lost.

3. *The world order*

This is the system that controls the thinking and behaviour of mankind. Satan masterminds it, and he is therefore called 'the prince of this world' (Jn 12:31; 14:30). His lieutenants in that spirit world are fallen angels, described as 'the rulers...the authorities...the powers of this dark world' (Eph 6:12). In contrast to 'the world of men', this is 'the world' that we are commanded *not* to love. If we do love it we do not have the love of God (1 Jn 2:15). It is the world that hated Christ and eventually crucified him, because he testified against its evil (Jn 7:7). It will likewise hate us because we side with Christ, and not with it (Jn 15:18–19).

In it—but not of it

1. *Why are we here?*

You will have noticed in our first reading that Jesus told his disciples, 'You do not belong to the world, but I have chosen you out of the world. That is why the world hates you' (v.19). We are like members of the Resistance in France during the Nazi occupation. Living under an alien rule, they felt at times like strangers in their own land. Perhaps you wonder, 'If, as Jesus says, the world hates us because we don't belong to the world, why doesn't God take us straight to heaven when we are born again?' One reason is that this very situation of conflict in which we are called to live is designed to shape us and make us what God wants us to be.

2.   Conformed or transformed?

The very thing God would use to make us, the devil can also use to mar us. The question is how we handle the conflict. Paul puts the issues squarely: 'Do not conform any longer to the pattern of this world, but be transformed by the renewing of your mind' (Rom 12:2). The believer in the world is either being conformed or transformed. Phillips translates this verse well: 'Don't let the world around you squeeze you into its own mould, but let God re-make you so that *your whole attitude of mind is changed.*' Whether we are conformed or transformed depends on our attitude of mind. The French Resistance fighter must have often been tempted in his mind to give in and conform. That was the easy way of escaping from the conflict. This is the greatest danger we face. We do not escape the temptation because we have been filled with the Spirit. We must heed fully what God says about our attitude and relationship with the world.

Two opposing kingdoms

That is, the world's and God's. Jesus said, 'My kingdom is not of this world' (Jn 18:36):

1.   The kingdom of this world

This is the world order that we have just been describing, which is totally antagonistic to the rule of God. Although energized and controlled by Satan, he has made rebel man—man without God—the centre of his empire. It is ruled by human wisdom and human reason (1 Cor 1:17–20). A characteristic of this kingdom is its *impermanence.*

It is passing away (1 Jn 2:17). Its rulers are coming to nothing (1 Cor 2:6). Those who live for it are tragically short-sighted. One day it will be destroyed for ever and the reign of Christ will take over (Dan 2:44; Rev 11:15).

2. The kingdom of God

In this sphere God is of course the centre. His revealed will, not human reason, is the rule and measure of all things. Men may only see and enter this kingdom by means of the new birth (Jn 3:3, 5). As we know, that involves changing sides, coming under God's rule and submitting to his new order. Before this we were motivated by 'the spirit of the world' in all our thinking, but now we have received 'the Spirit who is from God' (1 Cor 2:12), so that our lives have been radically re-orientated.

What is worldliness?

1. An inadequate concept

Christian tradition sometimes presents us with a view of worldliness that is not strictly biblical. It deals with externals but fails to touch the root of the matter. How a believer dresses, whether or not he indulges certain habits, engages in certain entertainments or pleasures, what he drinks, and what he permits himself to do on Sunday, will—according to this view—determine whether or not he is worldly. Such a believer *may* of course be worldly. But those who criticize him may be worldly in more serious areas. These externals are not the true criteria.

The scribes and the Pharisees had a similar list of rules by which they judged the piety of others. They were so careful about the trivial but overlooked the vital. They looked at the outside but neglected the inside. Jesus told them, 'You strain out a gnat but swallow a camel' (Mt 23:23–26). Those who are quick to judge their fellow Christians today by such external standards would do well to study a little more carefully what the Bible says.

2. The biblical concept

As we know, it is sadly possible to be born into God's kingdom, and yet behave as though we still belong to the world. 'You are still worldly. For since there is jealousy and quarrelling among you, are you not worldly? Are you not acting like mere men?' (1 Cor 3:3). This gives us the biblical concept of worldliness, *'acting like mere men'* instead of men who belong to God. Paul is not here speaking of how the Corinthian believers dress, or spend their leisure time, but of the more important matter of their relationships together, which were more characterized by 'the spirit of the world' than 'the Spirit who is from God'. In other versions of this passage you may find the word 'worldly' more literally rendered 'carnal' or 'fleshly', but it makes no difference because, as we shall now see, *carnality is worldliness*.

The Bible definition

'For everything in the world—the cravings of sinful man, the lust of his eyes and the boasting of what he has and does—comes not from the Father but from the world' (1 Jn 2:16). Scripture contains no definition of worldliness more comprehensive than this. It may touch body, mind or spirit.

1. Your body

If it is not under the rule of the Holy Spirit it will be ruled by 'the cravings of sinful man' ('the lust of the flesh',

RSV). This refers to the appetites of the body. They are God-given and good, but we must learn to rule them. If they rule us we are 'acting like mere men'—we are worldly. This word 'craving' (lust, desire) which occurs three times in 1 John 2:16–17, is the main characteristic of the world (note verse 17 especially). It is not confined to mere bodily appetites. Paul speaks of 'worldly passions' (Tit 2:12). It is the major motivation for all that the worldly man does.

2. Your mind

This finds its main satisfaction through 'the lust of the eyes'. The eyes are the main avenue to the mind. Consider the modern man's insatiable appetite for 'viewing' and spectating, and the massive industry that exists to satisfy it. It dominates his leisure time. He finds momentary satisfaction by being transported into an artificial and unreal world, which leaves him empty, and dissatisfied with his humble lot. Then his mind is bombarded with commercials to try to persuade him to buy on easy terms what he can't afford. He is ruled by the false philosophy that wealth is the secret of happiness, and that acquiring more and more of this world's goods will bring satisfaction. And so he craves. See what God says to him in Isaiah 55:1–2.

3. Your spirit

We are speaking here of the human spirit which, if it is not ruled by the Spirit of Christ will be ruled by 'the pride of life' (RSV) or 'the boasting of what he has and does' (NIV). This pride of life may also cause the worldly man to crave for money, not only to acquire material things, but for the popularity, prestige and worldly influence he believes it will bring. All this is the spirit of the world. Not only are many in the kingdom of God subtly influenced by it, but it even invades the work of God's kingdom. All competitiveness and rivalry has this spirit behind it. It lay behind the 'jealousy and quarrelling' of the Corinthian Christians that Paul said was worldly.

As you consider the above characteristics notice that they are all self-centred. We saw that that was the mark of the kingdom of this world. The man who truly lives for God's kingdom, however, is always Christ-centred (Phil 1:21).

The answer to worldliness

We have already seen that the New Testament is very clear in its commands. It says:

> Don't love the world (1 Jn 2:15).
> Don't be a friend of the world (Jas 4:4).
> Don't be conformed to the world (Rom 12:2).

But how can you live in the world without doing any of these?

1. Negatively

You can't do it by *rules and regulations*. This is the way of the scribes and Pharisees.

You can't do it by *escaping from the world*, so Jesus did not pray this for his followers, but that in a hostile world they would be protected (Jn 17:11–15). We are not called to a cloistered life, but to let our light shine before men (Mt 5:16).

You can't do it by *dealing with the externals*. 'O God, sweep away the cobwebs of pride, or jealousy, of selfishness in my life.' A brother used to weary everyone by praying after this fashion every week in the prayer meeting. One day someone cried out in the middle of his prayer, 'God, please kill the spider!' We must get to the root.

2. Positively

The only remedy for the spirit of the world in the life of the believer is the cross. We must view the world as a man would view it when nailed to the stake. That's what Paul says: 'May I never boast except in the cross of our Lord Jesus Christ, *through which the world has been crucified to me, and I to the world*' (Gal 6:14, italics mine). Though it may take on a thousand forms, worldliness is self-centredness instead of Christ-centredness. That's why the cross has to be the answer. We have dealt with this in Study 11, but we may now see new areas in which that teaching needs to be applied.

Memorize

> *Do not love the world or anything in the world. If anyone loves the world, the love of the Father is not in him. For everything in the world—the cravings of sinful man, the lust of his eyes and the boasting of what he has and does—comes not from the Father but from the world* (1 Jn 2:15–16).

Home task

1. Israel's deliverance from Egypt (a type of the world) by the blood of the Passover lamb is a parable of our salvation. It has been said, 'It was one thing to get Israel out of Egypt, but quite another to get Egypt out of Israel.'

(a) Note the different forms that their worldliness took on (1 Cor 10:1–10).

(b) How did God react? Note the things that happened to them.

(c) Could believers today who behave similarly experience the chastening of their heavenly Father? (10:11; 11:17–34).

2. In Scripture, worldliness is pollution. Believers are called upon:

(a) To come out and be separate (2 Cor 6:17–18).

(b) To keep themselves from being polluted (Jas 1:27; Rev 3:4).

Write down what you think these mean. Also what they do *not* mean (see notes under 'The answer to worldliness'). If there are areas in your life where you know that you have compromised with the world, confess this to God now, receive his cleansing and declare in faith that, through the cross, you are dead to the world and the world is dead to you.

For further study

1. Compare the three-fold definition of worldliness (memory verse) with:

(a) Eve's temptation in the garden (Gen 3:6).

(b) Our Lord's temptation in the wilderness (Lk 4:3–13).

Do you see a correspondence? What lessons should we learn from the woman's defeat and Christ's victory?

2. In Luke 17:26–36 Jesus likens the period preceding his return to 'the days of Noah' and the 'days of Lot'.

(a) Make a list of the characteristics of those days from the Genesis account.

(b) What is Jesus mainly emphasizing in verses 30–36 in

making this comparison? Can you find other scriptures
where Jesus gives the same warning?
(c) What is the lesson for us from Lot's wife (v.32)?

Salt and Light

Read
Matthew 5:13–16.

Introduction

In our last study we viewed the believer in the world from a negative viewpoint. The world was an alien society that could overwhelm and absorb him. He needed to watch lest he be corrupted and seduced by the love of the world. He must know that he belongs to another kingdom, and preserve his spiritual identity.

Now we must look at the positive and beneficial influence he may exert to affect the world around him. In Christ's words, his followers are 'the salt of the earth' and 'the light of the world'.

Significance of salt

To the oriental salt had two main uses:

1. For seasoning

'Is tasteless food eaten without salt, or is there flavour in the white of an egg?' (Job 6:6). So even Job liked salt with his egg! Salt gives flavour to what is otherwise insipid. Our conversation is tasteless if it is without spiritual seasoning (Col 4:6). Humanity is morally insipid. We cannot say to God, 'O taste and see that mankind is good,' for mankind is not only tasteless, but rotten.

2. For preserving

Salt is rubbed in to meat and fish to prevent them from going bad. In the days of Noah we read, 'Now *the earth* was corrupt in God's sight and was full of violence (Gen 6:11, italics mine). This could well be used to describe the twentieth century, but it was describing the days of Noah in the dawn of human history. This was the world that God visited with the judgement of the Flood. Noah and his family alone were righteous. They were the salt in their day. Had they been present in the earth in greater numbers they would no doubt have saved the earth from destruction. It was the same with Sodom. Had God found a righteous remnant of only ten people he would have saved the city (Gen 18:32). All this gives force to Jesus' statement here. He is saying that though the earth is corrupt, 'You are the salt [or preservative] of *the earth.*'

What God's salt is to do

1. It's not a permanent remedy

Salt is no final solution to decay. At best it can only delay the process. As salt we are not called to bring complete healing to human society. Christ's church is not a Human Improvement Society. We are to evangelize the world, but not to try to Christianize it. Scripture does not give us the expectation that evangelism will win over the whole of society, but rather that it will result in 'taking from [the world] a people' for God (Acts 15:13). It is important to be clear on this. The world is under judgement. 'Babylon the Great' is doomed to fall, never to rise again (Rev 17:18—18:3), and nothing will happen to change this. We are not looking for a paradise on earth, for it is destined to be destroyed by fire (2 Pet 3:10–13). Our citizenship and our inheritance are not earthly but heavenly (Phil 3:20; Heb 11:13–16).

2. *It must oppose sin*

We live in a world full of violence, greed, materialism, dishonesty and immorality. We are to be God's antiseptic in this putrifying carcase. Our standards are to be totally different. If the presence of a Christian has a restraining influence on profanity and smut in the place where he works, that Christian is salt.

'You're wanted on the phone,' said a Christian to his boss.

'Tell him I'm out,' was the reply.

The Christian picked up the phone. 'I'm sorry, sir, but the boss says he's out!'

Surprisingly, he wasn't fired, but nor was he ever asked to do it again. That man was salt. To God 'white lies' are black lies. With salt there is no compromise.

3. *It must be society's conscience*

Even in the 'enlightened' West there is injustice, inequality and selfishness. We are loud in our condemnation of apartheid, but within our own society there is discrimination on the ground of colour, lack of respect for the sanctity of life, the legalizing of abortion (a human life is slaughtered every three minutes in this country), a lobby for euthanasia and great pressure to permit the use of human embryos for scientific experimentation. Looking further afield, there are the prisoners of conscience, especially believers, behind the iron and bamboo curtains, and the starving millions of the Third World, and so much else.

Are Christians to try to influence society in these areas? A Spirit-filled church *will* inevitably do just that. Far-reaching social change has always come, even if not immediately, in the wake of spiritual revival. But there have always been the labours of individual Christians. Dedicated men and women like Shaftesbury, Wilberforce and Elizabeth Fry have changed the face of society. However, social action as such is not part of Christ's Great Commission to the church (Mt 28:18–20). That is confined to evangelism (which includes healing and deliverance, [Mt 10:8]) and the discipling of those who believe.

Social action is an individual matter. Some are particularly called to this, and they must know what part of this massive need they are to address. The church must always watch that it is not deflected from its major task of evangelism by the vast needs of suffering humanity. This has happened in the past with serious spiritual loss. Involvement in social action by believers does reflect the compassion of Christ, who fed the multitude as well as preached the good news to them, and may often pave the way for the reception of the gospel. 'You can't expect a man with no food in his stomach and no shirt on his back to listen to the gospel.' Jesus told his disciples to let the world see their good deeds (Mt 5:16), and Paul made reference to them in Titus 3:8, 14. The RSV renders verse 14, 'And let our people learn to apply themselves to good deeds, so as to help cases of urgent need, and not to be unfruitful.' Note that this is an appeal to the individual.

How salt works

1. It must be different

How could salt have any beneficial effect if it were the same in its nature as the meat, that is, subject to corruption? Salt and meat are in character diametrically opposed. This points to the nature of the new birth experience. Believers and unbelievers are as different as chalk from cheese. They are a different order of being (2 Cor 5:17). This is why we are told not to conform to the world (Rom 12:2). There is always pressure to do just that, and so be accepted. God calls his people 'holy' (1 Pet 2:9), which means set apart or different. But he also tells them, 'Be holy' (1 Pet 1:16), in other words, 'Be what you are.'

Jesus didn't say, 'Try to be the salt;' he said, 'You *are* the salt.' But he warned that it was possible for the salt to lose its saltiness, that is, for the Christian to lose his influence. The scientist would tell us that salt does not normally lose its saltiness. It is not affected, for example, by exposure to the elements. Probably it is only by excessive dilution that this can happen. For us, who are spiritual salt, the world is the diluting element. See how closely this theme is related to our last study. If we do not take heed to the things said there, worldliness will rob us of our distinctiveness, and so of our influence.

The American writer, Tom Sine, refers to this when he says, 'We have been remarkably effective at diluting Christ's extremist teaching and truncating his radical gospel.' Then speaking of America he goes on, 'That explains why we can have a nation of 200 million people, 60 million of whom profess to be Christian, and yet make such an embarrassingly little difference in the morality of our society.'

Here in Britain, though we do not have such a big proportion of professing Christians, the situation is the same. Our influence is minimal. Jesus told us to evangelize, and then to disciple (Mt 28:19–20; Mk 16:15). We have many converts but too few disciples. The disciple is always different. He is salty salt.

2. It must make contact

To be the conscience of society we must permeate society. To be the preservative of mankind we must mingle with mankind. 'You can't preserve fish by putting the fish in one barrel and the salt in the other.' In this, as in all else, our Lord Jesus is our perfect model. He lived no cloistered life. He could talk freely with Nicodemus the theologian, with Zacchaeus the tax collector or with the woman of 'easy virtue' that he met by a well. But in his mingling he never compromised his standards. Two statements concerning him, one by his critics and the other by the Holy Spirit, give us the perfect balance: the one said that he was 'a friend of... sinners' (Mt 11:19), the other that he was 'set apart from sinners' (Heb 7:26). If we are to be salt, like Jesus, we shall not allow ourselves to be *segregated from the world nor assimilated by the world*.

Significance of light

'You are the light of world' (Mt 5:14). Salt emphasizes more the believer's negative influence on the world, that is, counteracting corruption, while light emphasizes the positive.

A picture from creation

Many have seen that the creation account in Genesis 1 is a parable of salvation. It shows a world in chaos and darkness, like man without God. Then God said, 'Let there be light,' and the situation began to change. In verse 16 we read, 'God made two great lights,' referring to the sun and the moon: 'The greater light to govern the day and the lesser light to govern the night.' This corresponds to the two statements of Jesus, '*I am* the light of the world' (Jn 8:12)—he is the sun—and, '*You are* are the light of the world'—we are the moon. In the darkness of this age the church is to govern by being God's moon, and the only light we emit is the reflected light of the unseen 'Sun', who is at God's right hand. The New Testament confirms that ours is a borrowed light. We are not light in ourselves, we are only 'light in the Lord', because Christ has given us light (Eph 5:8, 14).

2. *What the light is to do*

It is only because God has imparted to us his life that we are the light of the world (Jn 1:4). Jesus goes on to speak of how the light is to be manifested in the life of his disciples: 'Let your light shine before men, that they may see your *good deeds* and praise your Father in heaven.' The Bible teaches us that we are not saved *by* good works but we are saved *for* good works, that is, we are saved to do them (Eph 2:8–10). They are the visible expression of the life God has put within us. They are the output of Christian character. They are not confined to doing good turns to neighbours. They are rather a demonstration of a totally different lifestyle. Such good deeds will mean at times our confessing Christ before men (Rom 10:9–10), witnessing to what he has done for us (Mk 5:19), giving a ready answer to those who ask us about our hope (1 Pet 3:15). Letting our light shine means influencing others by our lives and by our words.

3. Light is uncompromising

Just as salt reacts to corruption, light reacts to darkness.
It has no truck with darkness except to expose it (Eph
5:12–13). God is like that (1 Jn 1:5), and we are to be like
that too. 'For you were once darkness, but now you are
light in the Lord. Live as children of light (for the fruit of
the light consists in all goodness, righteousness and
truth)' (Eph 5:8–9). Almost every day we see and hear
things which are the fruit of darkness. They are the
normal fare on our TV screen. Have they become
acceptable practice to us? Paul warns us, 'Have nothing
to do with the fruitless deeds of darkness, but rather
expose them' (Eph 5:11). Turn over a stone, and all the
insects that live in the dark will scurry for their holes.
That's the effect that we are to have. We can seize the
initiative and put the enemy on the defensive.

4. It must be in the right place

The danger facing salt is to lose its saltiness, but the
danger facing light is to be put in a concealed place (Mt
5:15). There were secret disciples in Christ's day who for
fear of the authorities would not confess him (Jn 12:42–
43). They are still around. By failing to shine they rob
God of his due (Mt 5:16). They also rob the church, the
world and themselves. See what Christ says of them (Mt
10:32–33).

Memorize

*Let your light shine before men, that they may see your
good deeds and praise your Father in heaven* (Mt 5:16).

Home task

1. In what ways might a believer lose his saltiness? Don't merely quote scriptures like Romans 12:2 or Ephesians 5:11, but give practical examples of what these verses could refer to today.

2. In what ways might a believer hide his light instead of letting it shine? What might be the main reasons for doing this? What is the remedy?

3. Take time to examine your own life in the presence of God, and ensure that neither (1) nor (2) are true of you.

For further study

1. Consider the following statement: 'When believers understand their true function as salt and light, they will be preserved from a wrong view of what the Bible teaches about separation from the world' (see 2 Corinthians 6:17).
(a) What does that mean?
(b) Can you give scriptural examples of this wrong separation?
(c) Can you think of examples of it in the history of the church?

2. Jesus was speaking to a bunch of very ordinary men, most of them fishermen. He did *not* tell these humble disciples of his, 'You have some part to play in influencing the world for good and lighting its darkness.' He said, 'You are salt of the earth... you are the light of the world.'
(a) What does this teach us about the nature of Christianity in relation to other religions and philosophies of the world?

(b) Have these other religions any answers to a world in decay and darkness?

(c) Do they provide an alternative way to God? Quote scriptures for your answers.

On the Job

Read
1 Peter 2:13–21.

Introduction

Most people spend the bulk of their waking moments in secular employment. For some this is a drudgery and a bore. For many it is the constant scene of strife, with disputes and strikes over pay and working conditions. Growing numbers have been made redundant, or face the fear of it. Does the Bible give us 'a work ethic'? What has it to say about how we should perform our daily task?

God is our model

1. At work in creation

This is how the Bible story opens. After six days of activity '[God] rested from all his work' (Gen 2:2). Thus God has given to 'work' the concept of dignity, significance and value. He has taught us that seasons of labour need to be followed by times of rest. God pronounced his work 'very good' (Gen 1:31). So the first

Worker enjoyed 'job satisfaction', and his work was stamped with excellence. God did not sentence man to work because he fell into sin. He created man in his own image to be a worker too, to 'subdue' the earth (Gen 1:28), and then in the Garden of Eden, 'to work it and take care of it' (Gen 2:15).

2. Continuing to work

Having launched the universe on its course and placed man at the helm, God did not then leave him to get on with it. God continued to work. Jesus said, 'My Father is always at his work to this very day,' and then he added, 'And I, too, am working' (Jn 5:17). Jesus was implying that he took his cue from his Father. We must do the same. In the fourth Commandment God tells us to work as well as to rest, and pointed to himself as the model (Ex 20:9–11).

Importance of right attitudes

This is where the believer should stand out in sharp contrast to his unbelieving colleague. His whole attitude to his secular employment should be totally different. He is to have a kingdom 'workstyle', and this will be a powerful witness to Christ.

1. The unbelievers are watching

And if we are in secular employment, there is no place where they see more of us than at our place of work. So Peter exhorts us, 'Live such good lives among the pagans that, though they accuse you of doing wrong, they may see your good deeds and glorify God on the day he visits us' (1 Pet 2:12).

It was in an army barrack room that I was often accused. The men picked me up for anything I said or did that didn't measure up to their concept of a Christian. It kept me on my toes, and before long I saw that, despite my faults and failings, my lifestyle was making an impact.

2. Our attitude to the boss

Those watching us fasten on this at once. If it is negative, or if we fail to give 'full respect', all that we stand for may be compromised, for God's name and our teaching may be slandered (1 Tim 6:1). On the other hand, a right attitude of fidelity and trustworthiness towards those over us 'will make the teaching about God our Saviour attractive' (Tit 2:9–10). We will have more to say about this as we look at three very important areas where we need to watch our attitudes:

A right attitude to work itself

1. The attitude of society

The vast majority cannot think of work except in terms of money. Work is a necessary evil to be endured in order to earn enough to maintain a desired standard of living. Those who work hard and conscientiously, and who find enjoyment and fulfilment in their work are a diminishing segment of the work force. Those agitating for more pay for less work are on the increase.

On the wall of a business establishment I once read the following notice:

> Sometime between starting and quitting time, without infringing on lunch periods, coffee breaks, rest periods, story-telling time, holiday planning and the rehashing of yesterday's television programmes, we ask that each employee try to find some time for a work break!

2. *The true motivation*

That the average worker is joyless and unfulfilled is not primarily because his work is boring, but because his attitude to work is not right. It is the spirit of 'get' rather than 'give'. The Christian's primary motivation must be *serving*. This will dramatically change a person's whole approach to his work. He will no longer do his job half-heartedly with one eye on the clock and the other on the wage packet. This serving spirit within him will make him faithful, conscientious and hard-working.

3. *Serving which 'boss'?*

Does this concept of serving seem rather unreal in our modern society? 'I don't mind you telling me to serve Christ, but serving that so-and-so I work for...' In fact it *is* Christ we are talking about. Paul is telling believing slaves how they should obey their earthly masters, working with all their heart, and then he drops the bombshell to blow their resistance to smithereens: 'It is the Lord Christ you are serving' (Col 3:24). And if that was true in relation to working for an unscrupulous slave-owner of the first century, it is certainly true in relation to a twentieth-century employer.

A right attitude to money

1. *The worker and his wage*

Like every other member of society, the Christian must work to live. Jesus taught that 'the worker deserves his wages' (Lk 10:7). He is also responsible to support his dependents (1 Tim 5:8). What a worker should look for is 'a fair day's pay for a fair day's work'. But as we have been saying, money is not to be his primary motivation for working. What is commanded of an elder should be true of the believer in his secular job: 'Not greedy for money, but eager to serve' (1 Pet 5:2). The 'get rich quick' philosophy of modern man should have no place in the heart of the follower of Christ (1 Tim 6:9), and if, as often happens, God does prosper him, he is neither to set his heart on it (Ps 62:10), not to put his hope in it (1 Tim 6:17).

2. *The contented spirit*

Solomon tells us that 'all labour and all achievement spring from man's envy of his neighbour' (Eccles 4:4). He looks at what the other man has and becomes discontented. He's for ever trying to 'keep up with the Jones's'. John the Baptist told the soldiers who came to his baptism and professed repentance, 'Be content with your pay' (Lk 3:14).

God commands us, 'Keep your lives free from the love of money and be content with what you have' (Heb 13:5). This is an increasingly difficult command to keep in a world where we are bombarded with commercial propaganda designed to effect the very opposite in our thinking. There is, however, a legitimate money motive in working hard. It is to help the weak and give to the needy, as Jesus himself commanded us (Acts 20:35; Eph 4:28).

A right attitude to authority

In this the Christian's attitude will be as different from that of the world as in the two attitudes already discussed, for everywhere authority is being attacked and undermined.

1. *God delegates authority to men*

This is not only in the church but in the secular world. For example, governing authorities are established by

God, and we are commanded to submit to them—not
because they always act rightly or justly, but because
they are 'God's servants' to rule in the secular realm
Rom 13:1–5).

2. God delegates authority to employers

What the New Testament teaches about the master-slave
relationship applies now to the boss-worker relationship
in our modern society. It is clear that 'masters'
(employers) are viewed as acting for God, because we
are told to 'be subject' to them, and to 'try to please
them' (Tit 2:9). We are further told to do this 'with all
respect' (1 Pet 2:18).

3. Obey them as you obey Christ

This is exactly what Paul says (Eph 6:5). You will have
noticed that in our reading Peter does not confine this
submission to masters 'who are good and considerate,
but also to those who are harsh' (v.18). That's heavy
stuff, but read on and see what he says about the spiritual
value of 'unjust suffering' (vv.19–21). You will find
nothing in these passages about 'workers' rights', but
everything about how the Christian worker is to respond
to authority.

Does God then have no concern that employers should
be just and considerate? Yes, and we shall see what he
says to them in a moment. They are dealt with at another
level. All that he says to the Christian worker points
away from his taking action against an unjust boss. Sarah,
overtaken with jealousy, mistreated her slave girl Hagar
so that she ran away. But see what God said to Hagar
(Gen 16:8–9). This teaching is not nullified because
slavery is abolished in our society. This is the only
teaching in Scripture on how a worker is to relate to an
employer.

The marks of a Christian worker

Fulfilling the command to obey your earthly master 'just as you would obey Christ', and to serve him 'as if you were serving the Lord' (Eph 6:5, 7), will radically affect how you work, and whether you are fulfilled. It will not be difficult to work as the Bible exhorts us to:

1. With heart and soul

Solomon, a great and successful worker, said, 'Whatever your hand finds to do, do it with all your might' (Eccles 9:10). Paul says the same thing, but notice the motivation he gives for doing so (Col 3:23-24).

2. With fidelity

By our trustworthiness in material things we are qualifying to handle the 'true riches' (Lk 16:10–11). Christians are told 'not to steal from [their masters], but to show that they can be fully trusted' (Tit 2:10). But would a true believer steal? I have met those who seem to have no conscience about using office stamps or stationery for their own use, or stealing the boss's time by not giving him a fair day's work for their pay. Any unrighteousness may go unnoticed by our earthly boss, but not by our heavenly one (Col 3:25).

3. Without complaining or arguing

That's a tough one, but it's there, and it's an important aspect of our witness before a 'crooked and depraved generation' (Phil 2:14–15). It's an expression of true respect for authority, as is also the command 'not to talk back' (Tit 2:9).

4. Not to curry favour (to gain promotion)

You are to do what they want, 'not only when their eye

is on you and to win their favour, but with sincerity of heart and reverence for the Lord' (Col 3:22). So you work just as conscientiously when the boss is not around as when he is, because you are really working for another Boss—and he's always around (Gen 16:13; Phil 4:5).

A word to employers

1. The Judge stands at the door

He watches to see if there is fair play (Jas 5:9). James pronounces 'woe' on the rich in verses 1–6, men who have hoarded ill-gotten wealth at the expense of the poor. See what God said of a king who was unscrupulous towards his workers (Jer 22:13, 18–19). The cries of the oppressed always reach God's ears (Jas 5:4). He may bide his time, but he will act.

> Though the mills of God grind slowly, yet they grind
>   exceedingly small;
> Though with patience he stands waiting, with exactness
>   grinds he all.
>
> (Friedrich von Logau)

2. Be a do-gooder

Having told slaves, 'The Lord will reward everyone for whatever good he does,' Paul goes on to tell their masters, 'Treat your slaves in the same way' (Eph 6:8–9). The law even commanded a master to give a 'golden handshake' to a slave being freed (Deut 15:12–15). So the Lord carefully watches boss-worker relationships to reward each as they do good to the other.

3. Don't threaten

Ephesians 6:9 tells masters not to threaten their slaves as the rulers of the Jews threatened the apostles (Acts

4:21). A fair warning is justified, but threatening is a wrong use of authority. He who had all authority in heaven and on earth did not do this (1 Pet 2:23).

4. Give a square deal

'Provide your slaves with what is right and fair' (Col 4:1). This covers the whole area of pay and conditions. Note, the Christian employer is to act in the knowledge that his own 'Boss' in heaven is watching.

Memorize

> *Whatever you do, work at it with all your heart, as working for the Lord, not for men, since you know that you will receive an inheritance from the Lord as a reward. It is the Lord Christ you are serving* (Col 3:23–24).

Home task

'When it comes to work, some turn up their sleeves, and some turn up their noses.' The Bible calls the latter laziness. We are not speaking here of genuine unemployment, but of those who could work but don't, or who are lazy in their work.

1. Read the following scriptures and list all the things that characterize and accompany slothfulness: Proverbs 10:5; 24:30–31; 26:13, 16; Matthew 25:24–25; 2 Thessalonians 3:6–8, 11–12.

2. Read the following scriptures and make a list of all the encouragements to diligence and all the discouragements to slothfulness: Proverbs 6:9–11; 10:26; 12:24; 13:4; Ecclesiastes 10:18; Ephesians 6:7–8.

For further study

1. 'I'd rather have a man of the world as my employer than a Christian.' I have had believers say this to me. What do you think could be wrong with the attitudes of employer and/or worker to call forth such a remark? As well as the scriptures in the notes, look at 1 Timothy 6:2.

   2. Matthew 20:1–16 is a parable about unemployment and work. Why did some of the workers think the boss was unfair? What factors could have caused him to pay the later workers the way he did, and still fulfil his promise to pay them what was right (v.4)? What may we learn from this?

Pressing on Towards the Goal

Read
Hebrews 11:8–10, 13–16.

Introduction

In this final study we shall see that the only way to be living in this world as a mature Christian is to live for the next! Our goal must be heavenly, not earthly. We need to understand that we are 'strangers in the world' (1 Pet 1:1), impelled by a heavenly vision.

The world is passing

We have seen that salt is no permanent solution to decay. It only delays the process. As 'the salt of the earth' we can only delay corruption until God's purposes have been fulfilled. For the world, the sands of time are running out.

1. The natural world

It's like an old garment wearing out, soon to be changed and discarded (Ps 102:25–26). Men are tempted to think that 'nothing changes here', or in the words of Peter, 'Everything goes on as it has since the beginning of creation.' But they deliberately forget, Peter tells us, that the world has once been destroyed by water, and is finally to be destroyed by fire (2 Pet 3:4–7).

2. The world of men

This is also under judgement. The knowledge of this should be a great incentive to us to persuade men to believe on Christ, and thus escape from God's wrath (Jn 3:36). Noah was 'a preacher of righteousness' (2 Pet 2:5) who warned men of coming judgement, but they did not heed his warnings. As it was in the days of Noah, so it will be at the time of Christ's return (see Luke 17:26), only this time it will be a judgement of fire, not water (2 Thess 1:6–10).

3. The world system

It is obvious that this must also be doomed: 'The world and its desires pass away, but the man who does the will of God lives for ever' (1 Jn 2:17; see also 1 Corinthians 7:31). This puts mankind into two classes: those who live to fulfil their own desires, who are thus identified with the world system, and those who live to fulfil the will of God. The future of the one is grim, but the future of the other is glorious (Mt 25:46; 2 Thess 1:6–10).

How should this affect us?

'Since everything will be destroyed in this way, what kind of people ought you to be?' (2 Pet 3:11). A good question! Peter answers it along three lines:

1. Our living

'You ought to live holy and godly lives.' The knowledge that the world is to come to a fiery end should compel us to live lives that are pleasing to God. If we are different

176

in our nature from the world, and with a totally different destiny, surely we should be different in our lifestyle. That was a powerful statement when Peter wrote those words. How much more powerful now that we are nearly two thousand years nearer the event.

2. *Our outlook*

'Looking forward to the day of God.' We must be a forward-looking people. The future prospect of the world is one of 'doom and gloom', but ours is thrilling. We are looking forward to 'the glorious appearing of our great God and Saviour, Jesus Christ', when he will be finally vindicated. It is 'the blessed hope' of the Christian (Tit 2:13). And it should make us perpetual optimists.

3. *Our aim*

'To speed [or 'hasten' RSV] its coming.' We are not to wait passively for zero hour to strike. We have our part to play to bring that day nearer. Only God knows the full number of his chosen (2 Tim 2:19) whom he has given to his Son as his inheritance (Ps 2:8; Jn 6:37), but every conversion to Christ brings that final harvest nearer. As we play our part in the world as salt and light we inevitably 'speed its coming'.

Our status in the world

1. *A heavenly people*

Having been rescued from the dominion of darkness, we have entered the kingdom of heaven. We are therefore a colony of heaven, living on earth. Our thinking is now to be dominated by this unseen heavenly world, not by the seen world (2 Cor 4:18). We have received:

   (a) A heavenly vision. For Paul this happened on the

road to Damascus. A light brighter than the midday sun blinded him (Acts 22:11). It was symbolic of the glory that burst upon him, and left him blind to the dazzling sights of earth.

A business man saw a little child sucking a dirty stick of toffee. The child could not be persuaded to part with this until, presently, the man emerged from a sweet shop with a large slab of milk chocolate. There was no problem now in making him let go of the toffee. This has been called, 'The expulsive power of a new affection.'

Said Paul, 'Whatever was to my profit I now consider loss for the sake of Christ' (Phil 3:7). Paul 'was not disobedient to the vision from heaven' (Acts 26:19).

(b) A heavenly calling (Heb 3:1). Conversion is a right about turn, when we start moving in a new direction, propelled by a heavenly calling. Paul speaks of this as though he were an athlete, with a powerful motivation to go for gold: 'I press on towards the goal to win the prize *for which God has called me heavenwards in Christ Jesus*' (Phil 3:14, italics mine). What we experience here and now is but a foretaste of our heavenly inheritance. What starters is to the banquet.

Being a heavenly people means that we are:

2. *Strangers on earth*

Many young Christians have been distressed to find that their conversion has alienated them from their own family. That's how Christ felt (Jn 1:10–11, RSV). Conversion means a change of citizenship, from one that is earthly to one that is heavenly (Phil 3:20), and this inevitably brings a sense of alienation. The secular world has an increasing number of *displaced persons*, who for military, political or economic reasons have been uprooted, and are now without a homeland. The Christian is like that. The only difference is that he has no sense of loss, convinced that he has another and far better homeland awaiting him—and he's on his way.

3. The continuing conflict

The world is seeking to draw us. It wants to break down this sense of alienation and get us to conform (Rom 12:2). The world is uncomfortable with us as we are, and wants to assimilate us. Here is the conflict for the Christian, having to resist this perpetual influence. Jesus said, 'In this world you will have trouble. But take heart! I have overcome the world' (Jn 16:33). God could have evacuated us when we were converted. He could have airlifted us to our true homeland, as he will do one day (1 Thess 4:15–18). But this conflict is itself preparing us to reign with Christ in his coming kingdom (2 Tim 2:11–13; Rev 20:6).

Two contrasting characters

Abraham and his nephew Lot were citizens of Ur of the Chaldees. They turned their backs on its idolatry in response to a call of God, lured by the promise of an eternal city. Though they were wealthy, they became tent-dwellers in the land of Canaan.

1. Abraham

It is Stephen who gives us the key to this man's astonishing career: 'The God of Glory appeared to our father Abraham' (Acts 7:2). Abraham was sick and tired of Ur, and that day he caught a vision of a 'city with foundations'—which he knew Ur didn't have—'whose architect and builder is God' (Heb 11:10). That heavenly vision didn't simply spoil him for Ur, it spoiled him for earth. It turned him from a city-dweller into a tent-dweller (Heb 11:9). Of course there is no special virtue

in being a tent-dweller, but Abraham was called to
demonstrate something which should be true for every
Christian, that 'here we do not have an enduring city,
but we are looking for the city that is to come' (Heb
13:14). In pursuing this heavenly goal Abraham not only
became a giant of faith, 'the father of us all' (Rom 4:16),
but he had also the supreme honour of being the man in
Scripture whom God called 'my friend' (Is 41:8; cf Gen
18:17–19).

2. Lot

Lot never caught the vision that drew Abraham out of
Ur. He seemed to tag along, no doubt admiring his
uncle, and holding on to his coat tails (Gen 12:4; 13:1).
But you can't get very far on someone else's vision and
faith. Self-examination is needed (2 Cor 13:5). Lot is
described as 'a righteous man' (2 Pet 2:7), but because
he didn't have the heavenly vision he was compelled to
part company with his uncle (Gen 13:5–9). Abraham
couldn't pursue the heavenly calling with someone who
only had an earthly vision, even if he was righteous.

Lot, it seems, wasn't too sold on the tent-dwelling life
of Uncle Abraham. He didn't feel comfortable as 'a
stranger and an exile' in the land. Of the faith pioneers
we read, 'If they had been thinking of the country they
had left, they would have had opportunity to return
(Heb 11:15)—but they didn't. They were hooked. Tent-
dwelling or city-dwelling is not a matter of location but
of heart attitude. Lot was a man who had 'opportunity to
return', and took it. Why? His heart was not in the other
lifestyle. Faced with the choice he turned back, and soon
he was again a city-dweller—in a city even more wicked
than Ur. Consider the fatal steps he took:

'Lot looked up and saw...' (Gen 13:10). How we look
is vital.

'Lot chose for himself' (v.11). Material advantage was the motive.

'Lot...pitched his tents near Sodom' (v.12). Swim near the whirlpool and then:

'Lot...was living in Sodom' (14:12).

'Lot was sitting in the gateway of the city' (19:1). He had achieved a position of authority (Prov 31:23).

The world will always applaud the Lots. A man gets praise when he does well for himself (Ps 49:18). But in the end he lost everything—his wife, his home, his possessions, the chastity of his daughters and his self-respect (Gen 19). And it all sprang from a wrong choice—a choice that every Christian has to face throughout his life. There will always be 'opportunity to return'—for those who want to take it. Pioneers of the heavenly way are volunteers, not conscripts.

The prize of the heavenward call

1. The need of a goal

The more things we have to do the more we need envisioning and motivating. In the Philippian epistle Paul draws aside the curtain and shows us his inner life. We see what made him tick spiritually (3:12–14). We too need a goal that is more than a stimulus for immediate progress and personal fulfilment. It must be big enough to offset the back tow of the world, the flesh and the devil, and all that prevents us pressing on for the prize.

2. Forgetting what is behind

Paul knew that the memory of his past could hinder him. Many of us are hindered by our track record. 'Forgetting what is behind' (Phil 3:13). What do we need to forget?

Sin that we have confessed which God has forgiven,

but for which we haven't forgiven ourselves. Injured pride is usually the root. When we *humble* ourselves, *receive* God's forgiveness, and then *forget*, we are through.

The memory of mistakes and failures. Satan tells us that they disqualify us. He is a liar. See what kind of people God chooses (1 Cor 1:27–29). Praise God, we all qualify! We are old clay pots, weak and unworthy, so that it's all by God's grace, and God gets the glory (2 Cor 4:7, 15).

Living in the memory of past blessings. That can be a source of pride. We are wrongly limiting God, only expecting him to do in the future what we have seen him do in the past (see Ephesians 3:20).

3. Reaching out to take hold

Taking hold of what? 'That for which Christ Jesus took hold of me' (Phil 3:12). On the road to Damascus Paul was 'arrested' by the long arm of God's grace. He was never again free—to do his own thing. He was only free to do the will of the One who had arrested him. Our understanding of that purpose for which Christ took hold of us doesn't all come at once, it is a progressive revelation. To know God's will and do it was, for Paul, not a pastime but a passion. It was all bound up with knowing Christ, and he pursued it relentlessly. Everything else was 'rubbish' (Phil 3:8). It was the prize for which God had called him heavenwards (v.14).

But this was not just for Paul. He goes on say, '*All of us who are mature* should take such a view of things' (v.15, italics mine). Such an attitude to life is an indispensable mark of the mature believer. In striking contrast, note what he goes on to say about those whose 'mind is on earthly things' (vv.18–19).

4. The prize that awaits

Enlisting for the race doesn't secure the prize. There are
many competitors, but few prize-winners. 'I press
on...to win the prize.' In verse 8 he speaks of his desire
to 'gain Christ'. In this race, 'Christ is the path and Christ
the prize'. Gaining Christ could mean a deeper and more
intimate relationship with him. When he found himself
at last on 'the home straight' he had the assurance that he
had fully laid hold, and that the prize of the heavenward
call was his.

> The time has come for my departure. I have fought the good
> fight, I have finished the race, I have kept the faith. Now
> there is in store for me the crown of righteousness, which
> the Lord, the righteous Judge, will award to me on that day
> —and not only to me, but also to all who have longed for
> his appearing (2 Tim 4:6–8).

That last sentence could include you. The prize is not
just for the Pauls and other great characters, it's for
all—all who have had the heavenly vision, who have set
their affection on things above, 'who have longed for his
appearing'. This is what it means to be mature.

Memorize

> One thing I do: Forgetting what is behind and straining
> towards what is ahead, I press on towards the goal to
> win the prize for which God has called me heaven-
> wards in Christ Jesus (Phil 3:13–14).

Home task

1. An enterprising firm, learning that a sizeable proportion of the community were 'Bible-believing Christians', and eager to cash in on this market, decided to investigate in what way these people differed from the rest of the community, in lifestyle habits, likes and dislikes, etc. Their report? 'They are no different!'

(a) In what ways should citizens of heaven be different?

(b) As you note each point ask yourself, 'Am I different here?'

2. In pressing towards the goal for the prize, we spoke of the 'back tow' from the world around us.

(a) Make a list of the things you find the greatest hindrance and talk to God about them, claiming such promises as John 16:33; 1 John 4:4; 5:4.

(b) How would you help a Christian who feels he (or she) has never had 'the heavenly vision' (Jer 29:11–13; 33:3; Mt 7:7–8)?

For further study

1. Christians are called to be spiritually influential in the world. Someone has said, 'The world has been much more successful in influencing the church than the church has in influencing the world.' The story of Lot has something to teach us here.

(a) What do you think caused Lot to make the decision described in Genesis 13:10–11?

(b) Why do you think God allowed him to be carried away captive while living in Sodom, and then rescued by Abraham (Gen 14)?

(c) How did Lot's residing in Sodom affect his influence on the people around him (Gen 19:9, 14, 26, 31–36)?

(d) Study Lot's situation in the light of these scriptures:

1 Corinthians 15:33; 2 Corinthians 6:14–18; Ephesians 5:8–13.

2. Why does Hebrews 11 emphasize so strongly that these *men and women of faith* were also *characterized by possessing a heavenly vision* (see the reading)? What is the connection?

Living God's Way
A Course for Discipling New Christians

by Arthur Wallis

We live in a day of exciting growth, when churches are experiencing a new outpouring of the Holy Spirit and new believers are being gathered in.

The challenge is clear. Christians need to be firmly grounded in the truths of Scripture, so that they are equipped to give teaching and pastoral help to new believers.

This course has been specially designed for use in the local church setting, and is ideal for one-to-one discipling. With a clear and straightforward approach it covers the Bible's basic teaching so that the new Christian can gain a thorough understanding of Christian commitment and how it affects every area of life.

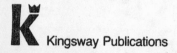

Kingsway Publications

God's Chosen Fast

by Arthur Wallis

Having proved over many years the great value and blessing of fasting, Arthur Wallis has written this book to share with us what the Bible says about this important and neglected subject. His aim is to deal not only with all the main passages in Scripture that touch on the matter, but also with the practical issues involved.

This is a balanced study which seeks to give to the subject the weight that Scripture gives it and to avoid exaggeration and over-emphasis. The book includes a biblical index, and an appendix dealing with the textual problems surrounding four references to fasting in the New Testament.

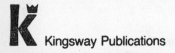
Kingsway Publications

Pray in the Spirit

by Arthur Wallis

In this book Arthur Wallis concentrates on the ministry of the Holy Spirit in relation to prayer, and investigates the full meaning of the apostle's injunction to 'pray in the Spirit'.

He analyses the spiritual and practical difficulties we encounter, and shows how the Holy Spirit helps us in our weakness and makes up for all our deficiencies. We are encouraged to yield ourselves completely to Him, allowing Him to pray through us.

As we enter into the 'deep things of God' unfolded here we shall discover a new power and effectiveness in our Christian lives.

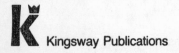

Kingsway Publications

Arthur Wallis:
Radical Christian

by Jonathan Wallis

'Arthur Wallis carved a way through the jungle of anti-charismatic evangelicalism. In this book you will read of his many achievements but also catch the heart of the man. Often seen on a platform as a rather formal conference speaker, or read as an authoritative author—here he can be viewed behind the scenes too. His warmth, love, joy and vulnerability come out of the shadows, as do the pains of his pioneering, the disappointments and the mistakes. These do not tarnish his story, but show a man of God, deeply committed to the Lord and the church, a man of deep spirituality and humanity. His story is of a man whose heart was touched by God; read it and yours will be touched too.'

— **Tony Morton**

'A man of God whose influence on my life has been profound.'

— **Michael Harper**

'Many of us wouldn't be in leadership without him, his writings and his example.'

— **Gerald Coates**

'His fathering role in the recent move of the Holy Spirit was unique. No one else had the breadth of relationships, or commanded respect in such a wide circle of believers.'

— **Terry Virgo**

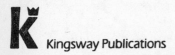

Kingsway Publications